FACE
Processing and Applications to Distance Learning

FACE
Processing and Applications to Distance Learning

Vuong Le
Amazon.com, USA

Pooya Khorrami
University of Illinois Urbana Champaign, USA

Usman Tariq
American University of Sharjah, UAE

Hao Tang
FX Palo Alto Laboratory, USA

Thomas Huang
University of Illinois Urbana Champaign, USA

World Scientific

NEW JERSEY • LONDON • SINGAPORE • BEIJING • SHANGHAI • HONG KONG • TAIPEI • CHENNAI • TOKYO

Published by

World Scientific Publishing Co. Pte. Ltd.

5 Toh Tuck Link, Singapore 596224

USA office: 27 Warren Street, Suite 401-402, Hackensack, NJ 07601

UK office: 57 Shelton Street, Covent Garden, London WC2H 9HE

Library of Congress Cataloging-in-Publication Data

Names: Le, Vuong (Computer scientist), author. | Khorrami, Pooya, author. | Tariq, Usman, author. | Tang, Hao (Computer scientist), author. | Huang, Thomas S., 1936– author.

Title: Face processing and applications to distance learning / Vuong Le (Amazon, USA), Pooya Khorrami (University of Illinois Urbana Champaign, USA), Usman Tariq (American University of Sharjah, UAE), Hao Tang (FX Palo Alto Laboratory, USA) & Thomas Huang (University of Illinois Urbana Champaign, USA).

Description: [Hackensack] New Jersey : World Scientific, 2016. | Includes bibliographical references.

Identifiers: LCCN 2015049551 | ISBN 9789814733021 (hc : alk. paper)

Subjects: LCSH: Optical pattern recognition. | Image processing. | Face perception.

Classification: LCC TA1650 .L45 2016 | DDC 006.4/2--dc23

LC record available at http://lccn.loc.gov/2015049551

British Library Cataloguing-in-Publication Data

A catalogue record for this book is available from the British Library.

Desk Editor: V. Vishnu Mohan

Typeset by Stallion Press

Email: enquiries@stallionpress.com

Printed in Singapore by Mainland Press Pte Ltd.

To our fellow lab mates at the IFP group

Preface

This book introduces the core problems of face processing, including facial shape modeling, biometrics, behavior analysis and animation. It also demonstrates the applications of the techniques in building a highly interactive distance learning systems.

For fundamental facial signal processing, we investigate the underlying techniques for analyzing the two factors contributing to facial visual appearance: shape and color texture. For the first aspect, the structure, motion and deformation of the facial shape are analyzed through 2D and 3D modeling and tracking from a variety of visual inputs such as image, video and depth signals. For the second aspect, a robust appearance model is used to investigate the variation of facial image patches through expressions of the subjects.

Based on these underlying techniques, we build a set of systems for biometrics and behavior analysis and apply them to distance learning applications. We introduce fundamental theory and practical approaches for real-time estimation of emotion and eye gaze from facial images and videos. These technologies are useful for gathering background, feedback and other information of online learning students during their sessions while protecting their privacy.

On the synthesis side, we present the research on reproduction of facial structure and deformation. Based on that, we build the system for synthesizing humanlike motion and expression on the subject's avatar. In a distance learning setup, these methods enable very-low-bit-rate video transmission of dynamic facial image of the instructor or virtual teaching agents to remote students.

Following the book, the readers will get a broad picture of the fundamental science of the field and at the same time investigate the technical details that make the research useful and interesting. We hope that the intellectual investigation motivated by the demand of real-life application will keep the book inspiring to current and prospective researchers and engineers in the fields of computer vision, machine learning and image processing.

Contents

Chapter 1

Introduction

Human faces are among the most important subjects of image processing, computer vision and graphics. Facial visual signal processing has been one of the top important research topics in the computer vision community. Research on face signal analysis and synthesis spans a broad range of modalities and methodologies including static frames and dynamic sequences of color images, depth images and LIDAR data. The applications of facial visual signal processing are also widespread including image enhancement, compression, recognition and animation. Recently, with the breakthroughs of computing infrastructure and social computing platforms, facial visual signal processing techniques are having tremendous opportunities in contributing to virtual reality, social network and remote sensing applications. The combination of facial processing techniques in graphics — such as face animation, and vision — such as expression recognition enables the unprecedented opportunity for remote and virtual interactive services.

Among the newest and most enthusiast adopters of facial processing techniques, modern remote learning platforms are making revolutionary changes in the world of education, especially in the form of Massive Open Online Courses. The interactive features on distance learning systems such as lecture delivering and student monitoring open great potential for providing rich, effective and efficient education services that surpass both traditional classroom setups and early online learning systems. These features essentially rely strongly on facial signal analysis and synthesis. This connection is at the center of the topics discussed in this book.

1.1 Motivation

The interactions between the participants of remote learning setup can be in two directions. In the presentation direction, the lecture and related content is transferred from the instructor's side to the students' side. In the feedback direction, at the students' side, the behavior and response of the audience will be estimated and conveyed back to the presenter.

In the current remote education platforms, most effort are put in the presentation direction with video streaming and content transferring systems. With the advance of video compression and streaming techniques, the webinar and teleconferencing style systems can deliver real-life video to remote audiences. However, those systems require high-end internetwork connections and do not support interactive content. The modern distance learning platforms need robust, efficient and interactive methods for delivering video, audio and other content to learners with diversified types of devices and networking infrastructure.

In the feedback direction, traditionally students' participation can only be monitored and responded directly by the instructor. This method is not efficient in the large classroom setup and impossible in remote online lectures. For modern online distant learning systems, effective feedback direction systems which observe and understand the participation of the remote learner is highly desired.

1.2 Overview

This book aims at providing a comprehensive and unified vision of facial image processing. It addresses a collection of state-of-the-art techniques which cover the important areas for facial biometrics and behavior analysis. At the same time, these techniques converge in serving practical applications of interactive distance learning.

We introduced the lecture delivering modules which support seamless 3D reconstruction and streaming of the instructor's facial motion to students through a photorealistic avatar. The facial structure, texture and motion are captured by a real time tracking algorithm. They are then encoded into a very low bit rate signal and efficiently transferred to a remote site where the full facial avatar is reconstructed and displayed.

At the students' side, a vision system is designed to observe and understand the participation of the users. We design the student site setup including a screen with the video cast from the instructor and a generic low-cost camera which captures the dynamics of student's appearance. These visual data are then analyzed by local and distributed vision algorithms for predicting facial expression and measuring the engagement level of the user.

The overview of the book is illustrated in Figure 1.1. In the first half of the book, from Chapter 2 to Chapter 5, we introduce the underlying facial processing techniques including expression recognition, 3D modeling and eye gaze estimation. In the later half, Chapter 6 and Chapter 7, we address the applications of these techniques in distance learning setup, namely model based video coding and student engagement monitoring.

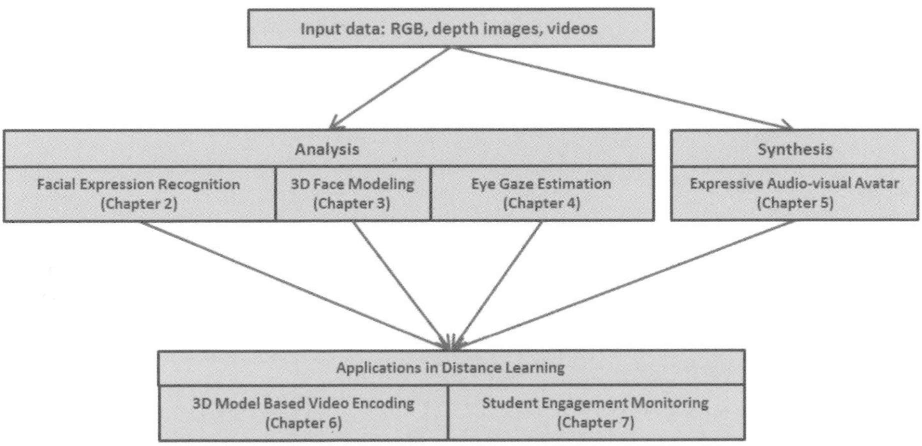

Fig. 1.1: Face processing and applications to distance learning.

Chapter 2

Facial Expression Recognition

2.1 Introduction

Automated facial expression recognition is beginning to have a sizeable impact in areas ranging from psychology to HCI (human–computer interaction) to HRI (human–robot interaction). For instance, there is an ever increasing demand to make the computers and robots behave more socially. Some example works that employ expression recognition in HCI and HRI are [Corive *et al.* (2001)] and [Kim *et al.* (2009)]. Another application for facial expression recognition is in computer-aided automated learning [Zeng *et al.* (2009)]. Here, the computer should ideally be able to identify the cognitive state of the student and then act accordingly. Say, if the student is not in high spirits, it may tell a joke. Apart from this, it can be very useful for online tutoring, where the instructor can get the affective response of the students as aggregate results in real time.

The increasing applications of expression recognition have invited a great deal of research in this area in the past decade. Psychologists and linguists have various opinions about the importance of different cues in human affect judgment [Zeng *et al.* (2009)]. But there are some studies (e.g. [Ambady and Rosenthal (1992)]) which indicate that facial expressions in the visual channel are the most effective and important cues that correlate well with the body and voice. This gives the motivation to focus on various face representations for facial expression recognition.

In the following, we review some of the existing literature for facial expression recognition.

2.2 Related Work

Most of the existing approaches do recognition on discrete expression categories that are universal and recognizable across different cultures. These generally include the facial expressions related to the six basic universal emotions: Anger, Fear, Disgust, Sad, Happy and Surprise [Zheng *et al.* (2012)]. This notion of the universal emotions with a particular prototype expression can be traced back to Ekman and his colleagues [Ekman *et al.* (1987)]. The availability of the corresponding facial expression databases have also made them popular with the computer vision community. A number of other works also focus on capturing the facial behavior by detecting facial action units[1] (AUs) as defined in the Facial Action Coding System (FACS) [Ekman (1993)]. The expression categories can then be inferred from these AUs [Littlewort *et al.* (2011)].

The choices of features employed for automated facial expression recognition are classified by Zeng *et al.* [Zeng *et al.* (2009)] into two main categories: geometric features and appearance features. In this section, we closely follow that taxonomy to review some of the notable works on the topic [Tariq *et al.* (2012a)].

The geometric features are extracted from the shape or salient point locations of important facial components such as mouth and eyes. In the work of Chang *et al.* [Chang *et al.* (2006)], 58 landmark points are used to construct an active shape model (ASM). These are then tracked to do facial expressions recognition. Pantic and Bartlett [Pantic and Bartlett (2007)] introduced a set of more refined features. They utilize facial characteristic points around the mouth, eyes, eyebrows, nose, and chin as geometric features for expression recognition. In a more holistic approach, Lucey *et al.* [Lucey *et al.* (2007)] utilize the Active Appearance Model (AAM) to analyze the characteristics of the facial expressions.

When sequences of images are available, one can also model the temporal dynamics of facial actions for expression recognition. For instance, Valstar *et al.* [Valstar *et al.* (2007)] propose to characterize speed, intensity, duration, and the co-occurrence of facial muscle activations in video sequences in a parameterized framework. They then decide whether a behavior is deliberate or spontaneous. Usage of temporal templates in [Valstar *et al.* (2004)], is another example. They used multilevel motion history

[1]There are groups of muscles on the face which move together. Their movement signifies the presence/absence of a particular AU. For instance, AU02 signifies 'Outer Brow Raiser,' etc.

images to study the subtle changes in facial behavior in terms of action units.

The appearance features representing the facial characteristics such as texture and other facial miniatures are also employed in many works. Among them, another work of Bartlett and colleagues [Bartlett *et al.* (2003)] uses Gabor wavelets which are extracted after warping 3D images into canonical views. Also, the work by Anderson and McOwan [Anderson and McOwan (2006)] introduces a holistic spatial ratio face template. In this work, the movement of identified regions of the face are extracted and separated from rigid head movement through tracking and used as features for support vector machine (SVM) classification.

A work by Hu *et al.* [Hu *et al.* (2008b)] details multi-view expression recognition using appearance features. They extract three kinds of local patch descriptors: Histogram of Oriented Gradients (HOG), Local Binary Patterns (LBP), and Scale-Invariant Feature Transform (SIFT). They then apply Locality Preserving Projection (LPP) for dimensionality reduction followed by SVMs for classification. Their method shows good recognition results on a publicly available database. SIFT has also been used in some other works. For instance, Berretti *et al.* [Berretti *et al.* (2010)] extract SIFT descriptors on a set of landmarks on depth images for SVM classification. Other features like Pyramid of Histogram Of Gradients (PHOG) and Local Phase Quantization (LPQ) have also been used for expression recognition, for instance in [Dhall *et al.* (2011)]. Yang and Bhanu [Yang and Bhanu (2011)] report better performance with LPQ than LBP for emotion classification.

Besides geometric and appearance based, the hybrid features have also been used. They have shown impressive recognition results. In [Tian *et al.* (2001)], Tian *et al.* combined shapes and the transient features to recognize fine-grained changes in facial expressions. Several other works, such as [Tang and Huang (2008a)] and [Tang and Huang (2008b)], follow the traditional approach of using 3D face models to estimate the movements of the facial feature points. These features capture facial Action Units (AUs). Their presence/absence can also describe the overall facial expression of a subject.

It is worthwhile to point out that much of the literature focuses on expression recognition from frontal or near-frontal face images [Zeng *et al.* (2009); Zheng *et al.* (2012)]. Expression recognition from non-frontal faces is much more challenging. It is also of more practical utility, since it is not trivial in real applications to always have a frontal face. Nonetheless, there are only a handful of works in the literature working with non-frontal faces.

The works on non-frontal view expression recognition can also be classified based upon the types of features employed. Some works use geometric features: e.g., Hu *et al.* [Hu *et al.* (2008a)] and Rudovic *et al.* [Rudovic *et al.* (2010b,a)] use displacement or mapping of manually labeled key points to the neutral or frontal face views of the same subject. In contrast, some researchers extract various low-level features (e.g., SIFT) on pre-labeled landmark points and use them for further processing [Zheng *et al.* (2012)]. Some of such works include those by Hu *et al.* [Hu *et al.* (2008b)] and Zheng *et al.* [Zheng *et al.* (2009)].

Note that the aforementioned approaches, for non-frontal view expression recognition, require the facial key-points location information, which needs to be pre-labeled. However, in real applications, key-points need to be automatically detected, which is a big challenge itself in the case of non-frontal faces, and this problem can be amplified in low-quality images. To address this issue there have been some attempts which do not require key-point locations; they rather extract dense features on detected faces.[2] The prominent examples in this category include works by Moore and Bowden [Moore and Bowden (2009, 2011)], Zheng *et al.* [Zheng *et al.* (2010)] and Tang *et al.* [Tang *et al.* (2010)]. Moore and Bowden [Moore and Bowden (2009, 2011)] extract LBP features and their variants from non-overlapping patches, while Zheng *et al.* [Zheng *et al.* (2010)] and Tang *et al.* [Tang *et al.* (2010)] extract dense SIFT features on overlapping image patches. Zheng *et al.* [Zheng *et al.* (2010)] use regional covariance matrices for the image-level representation. Tang *et al.* [Tang *et al.* (2010)], after dense feature extraction, represent the images with super vectors which are learned based on ergodic hidden Markov models.

It is worthwhile to mention that the Binghamton University 3D Facial Expression (BU3D-FE) database [Yin *et al.* (2006)] has become the de-facto standard for works in the area of non-frontal view expression recognition. Many works use five pan angle views rendered from the database (0°, 30°, 45°, 60° and 90°) [Hu *et al.* (2008b,a); Zheng *et al.* (2009); Moore and Bowden (2009, 2011)]. However, in real-world situations, we have variations in both pan and tilt angles. Thus, in more recent works [Zheng *et al.* (2010); Tang *et al.* (2010)], people are working with a range of both pan and tilt angles.

In this chapter, we primarily focus on image-based facial expression recognition with an emphasis on non-frontal faces. We present two super-

[2] Extraction of dense features essentially implies computing features on an entire image region from overlapping or non-overlapping image patches.

vised image descriptor models employed for this purpose. The presented models are inspired from the very popular Bag-of-Words image classification framework. We use Gaussian Mixture Models (GMMs) as 'dictionaries' to come up soft estimates in Soft Vector Quantization (SVQ); while in Super-Vector Encoding (SVE), we use them to come up with image-specific distributions. Our contribution is to learn these GMMs in a supervised manner using class information such that they are better suited for classification. We term these supervised models respectively as Supervise Soft Vector Quantization (SSVQ) [Tariq *et al.* (2013)] and Supervised Super-Vector Encoding (SSE) [Tariq *et al.* (2014)].

Recent years have seen a growing interest in supervised dictionary learning in general. Such approaches may be classified into the following four categories [Lian *et al.* (2010)].

The first category deals with computing multiple dictionaries. The work by Perronnin [Perronnin (2008)] and Zhang *et al.* [Zhang *et al.* (2009)] comes under this category. The second type comprises the works which learn dictionaries by modifying an initial dictionary under various criteria, for instance by using mutual information to merge visual words [Fulkerson *et al.* (2008)]. Another criterion may be the intra-class compactness and inter-class discrimination power [Winn *et al.* (2005)]. However since only the merging process is considered, one has to begin with a large enough dictionary so that it contains sufficient discriminative power to begin with.

The third category learns a dictionary by working with descriptor-level discrimination. However, as noted in [Lian *et al.* (2010)], this assumption is quite strong because of the overlap amongst local regions of images from different categories. Some example works in this category are [Lazebnik and Raginsky (2009)], [Shotton *et al.* (2008)], [Mairal *et al.* (2009)] and [Mairal *et al.* (2008)].

The fourth class of algorithms learn the descriptor models/dictionaries with image-level discriminative criteria. Previous example works in this category include [Lian *et al.* (2010)] and [Yang *et al.* (2010)]. Our presented work on SSVQ and SSE [Tariq *et al.* (2013)], [Tariq *et al.* (2014)], [Tariq (2013)] also falls into this category. Unlike the work in [Lian *et al.* (2010)], we employ soft assignment coding in SSVQ to encode an image with a Gaussian Mixture Model, which can better describe the underlying multi-modal distribution of the local descriptors. The work on SSE follows the similar core idea, but linking the descriptor model to the image level representation is not straightforward anymore. We use differentiable logistic loss function for each of the SSVQ and SSE algorithms. Thus, our objective function is differentiable without any conditions, while [Lian *et al.* (2010)] relies on sub-gradient and [Yang *et al.* (2010)] has to make some assumption for computing the gradient. Our results on SSVQ and SSE show significant improvement compared to SVQ and SVE.

In the following we will start with the description on "mid-level" level features, SVQ and SSE. It is then followed by the presentation of SSVQ and SVE algorithms.

2.3 Image Features

Good and relevant features are detrimental in any computer vision algorithm. In image classification, many methods first extract low-level features at key-points or over a dense grid in an image [Boureau *et al.* (2010)]. Examples of such low-level features include Scale-Invariant Feature Transform (SIFT) Feature, Local Binary Pattern (LBP) features, Discrete Cosine Transform Features (DCT), etc. These local features, in general, are then combined into image-level representations [Boureau *et al.* (2010)]. We term these image-level representations as "mid-level" features [Boureau *et al.* (2010)]. In the following we shall review briefly the mid-level image representations on top of which we developed their supervised counter-parts.

2.3.1 *Mid-Level Features*

The low-level features may be combined in various ways to give image level descriptors. One way may be to concatenate them together. However, this may lead to very high dimensional feature vectors. Also such image-level features may be seriously prone to image misalignments. The approaches used in practice for mid-level feature representation typically follow a common structure that consists of three computational modules [Tariq *et al.* (2012b)]; local feature extraction, descriptor encoding and spatial feature pooling. With these mid-level feature representations, state-of-the-art recognition performances have been reported in object recognition and scene classification tasks on various benchmark datasets, such as Caltech-101 [Fei-Fei *et al.* (2007)], Caltech-256 [Griffin *et al.* (2007)] and Scene 15 [Lazebnik *et al.* (2006)]. In the following we describe the mid-level feature representations relevant to the chapter.

2.3.1.1 *Soft Vector Quantization*

In the recent past, *Bag of Words* (BoW) model has been very popular in image categorization. In this approach, features extracted from unordered patches from images are quantized into discrete *visual words* (code-book). These *visual words* are then used to compute a compact histogram representation of each image, which is then used for classification [Tariq and Huang (2012)].

Suppose, $S = \{I^d, c^d\}_{d=1}^{D}$ is a corpus of images, where $I^d = \{z_1^d, \ldots, z_{N_d}^d\}$ represents the dth image, z_i^d are the feature vectors extracted from I^d and $c_d \in \{c_1, \ldots, c_M\}$ are labels in a multi-class case. Let $V = \{v_1, v_2, \ldots, v_k\}$ be a matrix whose columns represent visual words. For (hard) Vector Quantization (VQ), the feature vector z_i^d from the dth image can be represented as a K-dimensional vector ϕ_i^d, where

$$\phi_i^d[k] = \begin{cases} 1 & \text{if } k = \arg\min_l \left\| z_i^d - v_l \right\|_2, \\ 0 & \text{otherwise.} \end{cases} \tag{2.1}$$

However, the hard assignment in Eq. 2.1 may be too restrictive. Also, hard VQ may lead to greater representation/reconstruction errors. One can use a Gaussian Mixture Model (GMM) to arrive at Soft Vector Quantization (SVQ) instead. Given a set of training images, GMM can be learned by the Expectation Maximization (EM) algorithm [Bishop (2006)].

Thus, given a GMM (with K components and parameters $\Theta = \{\pi_1, \ldots, \pi_K; \mu_1, \ldots, \mu_K; \Sigma_1, \ldots, \Sigma_K\}$), the likelihood of a p-dimensional feature vector z_i^d is given as

$$p(z_i^d|\Theta) = \sum_{k=1}^{K} \pi_k \mathcal{N}(z_i^d; \mu_k, \Sigma_k). \tag{2.2}$$

In SVQ, we may represent the feature vector z_i^d as ϕ_i^d, where

$$\phi_i^d[k] = \frac{\pi_k \mathcal{N}(z_i^d; \mu_k, \Sigma_k)}{\sum_{j=1}^{K} \pi_j \mathcal{N}(z_i^d; \mu_j, \Sigma_j)} \tag{2.3}$$

or equivalently,

$$\phi_i^d[k] = p(k|z_i^d). \tag{2.4}$$

The image level descriptor can then be represented by a histogram computed from all the $\phi_i^d, i \in 1, \ldots, N_d$, or in other words mean pooling across the image,

$$\Phi^d = \frac{1}{N_d} \sum_{i=1}^{N_d} \phi_i^d, \tag{2.5}$$

where N_d is the number of low-level feature vectors extracted from the image I^d.

This image-level descriptor can then be used for classification. However, please note that such descriptors discard the spatial information in the patches extracted from various regions of an image. Hence to address this issue, *Spatial Pyramid Matching* (SPM) was proposed in [Lazebnik *et al.* (2006)]. In this framework, the given image is partitioned into various sections on various scales and then the BoW histograms are extracted for each of these partitions. These histograms are then concatenated together into one feature vector which is then used for classification. SPM has made tangible success on various image categorization databases like Caltech-101 [Fei-Fei *et al.* (2007)] and Caltech-256 [Griffin *et al.* (2007)]. It had been found empirically that the BoW model and SPM both give significantly better performance when used in conjunction with a non-linear kernel, e.g. *intersection kernel* or *chi-square kernel*, compared to when used with a linear kernel.

2.3.1.2 *Super-Vector Encoding (SVE)*

The Super-Vector Encoding (SVE) [Zhou *et al.* (2009)] representation is a locality sensitive patch-based approach. Here the patch locality information is characterized jointly with the appearance information. It is robust to partial occlusion and misalignment scenarios. This image representation is fairly general and can be used for any object recognition task. We follow [Zhou *et al.* (2009)] for its brief derivation.

In the process of extracting these features, we first extract overlapping image patches. Then we extract any low-level descriptors for each patch (SIFT, DCT, etc.). Then we learn a Gaussian Mixture Model (GMM), on the feature vectors extracted from patches, for the whole corpus. We term this GMM as the Universal Background Model (UBM). Please note that, given a set of training samples, a GMM can be learned through the Expectation Maximization (EM) algorithm. EM finds the maximum likelihood estimates of the parameters of a GMM is an iterative fashion. Further details of EM can be found in [Bishop (2006)].

The UBM works as a reference across different images. We use this UBM to learn image-specific GMMs by MAP adaptation. SVE features are essentially the super-vectors constructed from the parameters of the image-specific GMM. This gives us the overall appearance information for that image.

The location information can then be encoded in SVE features by either using *Gaussian maps* as in [Zhou *et al.* (2009)], or by repeating the same process on a spatial pyramid structure (SPM). The resulting SVE features on different sections can then be concatenated together. Or alternatively, we can append the low-level features with the xy-patch locations of the patches from which they are extracted. This gives comparable performance to Gaussian maps or SPM, as we later discovered in our experiments.

If z_i^d denotes the i-th p-dimensional feature vector from the d-th image. Then we can model z_i^d by a GMM,

$$p(z_i^d|\Theta^d) = \sum_{k=1}^{K} \pi_k^d \mathcal{N}(z_i^d; \mu_k^d, \Sigma_k^d), \tag{2.6}$$

where $(\pi_k^d, \mu_k^d, \Sigma_k^d)$ are the image-specific weight, mean and covariance matrix of the kth Gaussian component, respectively and K denotes the total number of Gaussian components. We restrict the covariance matrices Σ_k^d to be a diagonal matrix, Σ_k, shared by all images, for computational reasons.

The image specific parameters are learnt through *Maximum A Posteriori* (MAP) adaptation by maximizing the following via EM,

$$\max_{\Theta} \left[\ln p(z_i^d|\Theta) + \ln p(\Theta)\right].$$

In the E-step, we find

$$p(k|z_i^d) = \frac{\pi_k \mathcal{N}(z_i^d; \mu_k, \Sigma_k)}{\sum_{j=1}^{K} \pi_j \mathcal{N}(z_i^d; \mu_j, \Sigma_j)} \tag{2.7}$$

and

$$n_k = \sum_{i=1}^{N_d} p(k|z_i^d) \tag{2.8}$$

and in the M-step, we update

$$\pi_k^d = \gamma_k \frac{n_k}{N_d} + (1-\gamma_k)\pi_k, \tag{2.9}$$

$$\mu_k^d = \alpha_k m_k + (1-\alpha_k)\mu_k, \tag{2.10}$$

where

$$\begin{aligned} m_k &= \frac{1}{n_k}\sum_{i=1}^{N_d} p(k|z_i^d) z_i^d, \\ \alpha_k &= \frac{n_k}{(n_k+r)}, \quad \gamma_k = \frac{N_d}{(N_d+T)}. \end{aligned} \tag{2.11}$$

Note that N_d is the number of patches extracted from the image. One can note that if a Gaussian component has a high probabilistic count, n_k, then α_k approaches 1 and the adapted parameters emphasize the new sufficient statistics m_k; otherwise, the adapted parameters are determined by the global model μ_k. Here r and T are the tuning parameters. They also affect the MAP adaptation. The larger r and T, the larger the influence of the prior distribution on the adaptation. In practice we adjust r and T empirically [Zhou *et al.* (2009)].

After adaptation, we can calculate the similarity between a pair of images via the similarity between two GMMs. In our experiments, we follow the suggestion in [Zhou *et al.* (2008)] and choose the super-vector for an image, I^d, to be

$$\Psi^d = \left[\sqrt{\pi_1^d}\Sigma_1^{-\frac{1}{2}}\mu_1^d, \ldots, \sqrt{\pi_K^I}\Sigma_K^{-\frac{1}{2}}\mu_K^d\right]^T. \tag{2.12}$$

2.4 Supervised Image Descriptor Encoding

In this section we present the formulation of Supervised Soft Vector Quantization (SSVQ) and Supervised Super-vector Encoding (SSE) [Tariq *et al.* (2013)], [Tariq *et al.* (2014)], [Tariq (2013)]. The basic idea in both of these is similar, however, the formulation is very different. We aim to encode discriminatory information in UBM learning by encoding class information by linking the classification loss to the learning process.

2.4.1 *Supervised Soft Vector Quantization (SSVQ)*

The basic idea in Supervised Soft Vector Quantization (SSVQ) is to reduce the loss function in a classifier, given a training set, by modifying the image descriptor model (which is a GMM in our case). We use logistic regression in our framework. The loss function for ℓ^2-regularized logistic regression can be given as [Fan *et al.* (2008)]

$$L = \frac{1}{2}(w^T w) + A \sum_{d=1}^{D} \log(1 + \exp[-c^d w^T \Phi^d]). \tag{2.13}$$

Here, A is a scalar, pre-selected by cross-validation on the training set. The derivative of L w.r.t. μ_k can be written as

$$\frac{\partial L}{\partial \mu_k} = A \sum_{d=1}^{D} \frac{-c^d \exp[-c^d w^T \Phi^d]}{1 + \exp[-c^d w^T \Phi^d]} w^T \frac{\partial \Phi^d}{\partial \mu_k}. \tag{2.14}$$

To compute the derivative in Eq. 2.14, we need to compute the derivative for each ϕ_i^d,

$$\frac{\partial \Phi^d}{\partial \mu_k} = \frac{1}{N_d} \sum_{i=1}^{N_d} \frac{\partial \phi_i^d}{\partial \mu_k}. \tag{2.15}$$

Note that

$$\frac{\partial \phi_i^d}{\partial \mu_k} = \left[\ldots, \frac{\partial \phi_i^d[k]}{\partial \mu_k}, \ldots, \frac{\partial \phi_i^d[m]}{\partial \mu_k}, \ldots\right]^T, \quad \text{where } m \neq k. \tag{2.16}$$

Now consider from Eq. 2.3,

$$\begin{aligned} \frac{\partial \phi_i^d[k]}{\partial \mu_k} &= \frac{\partial}{\partial \mu_k}\left[\frac{\pi_k \mathcal{N}(z_i^d; \mu_k, \Sigma_k)}{\sum_{j=1}^{K} \pi_j \mathcal{N}(z_i^d; \mu_j, \Sigma_j)}\right] \\ &= \frac{\partial p(k|z_i^d)}{\partial \mu_k}. \end{aligned}$$

After some derivation we get

$$\frac{\partial \phi_i^d[k]}{\partial \mu_k} = (p(k|z_i^d) - (p(k|z_i^d))^2)[z_i^d - \mu_k]^T \Sigma_k^{-1}.$$

Using Eq. 2.4 we get

$$\frac{\partial \phi_i^d[k]}{\partial \mu_k} = (\phi_i^d[k] - (\phi_i^d[k])^2)[z_i^d - \mu_k]^T \Sigma_k^{-1}. \tag{2.17}$$

Similarly for the case when $m \neq k$, we have

$$\begin{aligned}\frac{\partial \phi_i^d[m]}{\partial \mu_k} &= \frac{\partial}{\partial \mu_k}\left[\frac{\pi_k \mathcal{N}(z_i^d;\mu_m,\Sigma_m)}{\sum_{j=1}^{K}\pi_j \mathcal{N}(z_i^d;\mu_j,\Sigma_j)}\right]\\ &= \frac{\partial p(m|z_i^d)}{\partial \mu_k}\\ &= -p(k|z_i^d)p(m|z_i^d)[z_i^d-\mu_k]^T\Sigma_k^{-1}.\end{aligned}$$

And this essentially implies

$$\frac{\partial \phi_i^d[m]}{\partial \mu_k} = -\phi_i^d[k]\phi_i^d[m][z_i^d-\mu_k]^T\Sigma_k^{-1}. \tag{2.18}$$

Please note that each of Eqs. 2.17 and 2.18 represents a $1\times p$ vector, where p is the dimension of μ_k. Thus, $\frac{\partial \phi_i^d}{\partial \mu_k}$ is a $K \times p$ matrix, where K is the number of mixtures in GMM.

Equations 2.17 and 2.18 are then used to compute $\frac{\partial \Phi_i^d}{\partial \mu_k}$ in Eq. 2.15. Stochastic gradient descent with online learning can be used to update $\mu_k, k \in \{1,\ldots,K\}$ as in [Tariq *et al.* (2013)] and [Tariq (2013)].

$$\mu_k^{(t+1)} = \mu_k^{(t)} - \lambda^{(t)}\left(\frac{\partial L^d}{\partial \mu_k}\right)^T, \tag{2.19}$$

where

$$\frac{\partial L^d}{\partial \mu_k} = A\frac{-c^d}{1+\exp(c^d w^T\Phi^d)}w^T\left(\frac{\partial \Phi^d}{\partial \mu_k}\right), \tag{2.20}$$

$$\lambda^{(t)} = \frac{\lambda^{(t_0)}}{\sqrt{n/N_d+1}}. \tag{2.21}$$

2.4.2 *Multi-class SSVQ*

Suppose we have a multi-class problem with $M > 2$ classes. Then we can have M regressors, trained in a one-vs-rest (OVR) fashion. The motivation for the OVR setting is that it is efficient, requires less computation and performs comparably to other multi-class classifier learning methodologies [Fan *et al.* (2008)]. Now the regressors may be arranged in an $M\times K$ matrix W. Thus the derivative of the loss function in the multi-class setting for a single training sample can be given as (derived from Eq. 2.20)

$$\frac{\partial L^d}{\partial \mu_k} = A \sum_{i=1}^{M} \frac{-y[i]}{1+\exp(y[i]W[i,:]^T \Phi^d)} W[i,:] \left(\frac{\partial \Phi^d}{\partial \mu_k} \right), \tag{2.22}$$

where

$$y[i] = \begin{cases} +1 & \text{if } \Phi^d \in i^{th} \text{ class,} \\ -1 & \text{otherwise,} \end{cases}$$

$$W[i,:] = \text{ regressor trained on } i^{th} \text{ class vs rest.}$$

Stochastic gradient descent is then used with online learning to update μ_k, $k \in \{1, \ldots, K\}$ in a similar fashion as for the binary class problem. Finally, Eqs. 2.3 and 2.5 are used to compute the image-level descriptors using the new discriminative GMM with updated means, which are then used for training and testing.

2.4.3 *Supervised Super-Vector Encoding (SSE)*

As pointed out earlier, the aim here is again to learn the GMM in a discriminative fashion by connecting the classification loss with SVE features to the GMM learning process.

Similar to SSVQ, we use logistic regression in our framework [Tariq *et al.* (2014)]. The loss function for ℓ^2-regularized logistic regression with SVE feature Ψ^d can be given by ([Fan *et al.* (2008)]),

$$L = \frac{1}{2}(w^T w) + A \sum_{d=1}^{D} \log(1+\exp[-c^d w^T \Psi^d]) \tag{2.23}$$

here A is the regularization parameter (found beforehand with cross-validation on the training set). The derivative of L w.r.t. μ_k can be written as,

$$\frac{\partial L}{\partial \mu_k} = A \sum_{d=1}^{D} \frac{-c^d \exp[-c^d w^T \Psi^d]}{1+\exp[-c^d w^T \Psi^d]} w^T \frac{\partial \Psi^d}{\partial \mu_k}. \tag{2.24}$$

Now if Ψ^d is given by,

$$\Psi^d = \left[\ldots, \sqrt{\pi_k^d} \Sigma_k^{-\frac{1}{2}} \mu_k^d, \ldots, \sqrt{\pi_m^d} \Sigma_m^{-\frac{1}{2}} \mu_m^d, \ldots \right]^T, \tag{2.25}$$

where, $k \neq m$, then the derivative of Ψ^d w.r.t. μ_k is given by,

$$\frac{\partial \Psi^d}{\partial \mu_k} = \left[\ldots, \frac{\partial [\sqrt{\pi_k^d} \Sigma_k^{-\frac{1}{2}} \mu_k^d]}{\partial \mu_k}, \ldots, \frac{\partial [\sqrt{\pi_m^d} \Sigma_m^{-\frac{1}{2}} \mu_m^d]}{\partial \mu_k}, \ldots \right]^T, \tag{2.26}$$

where $m \neq k$. After derivation[3] we arrive at the following equations,

$$\frac{\partial}{\partial \mu_k}\left(\sqrt{\pi_k^d}\Sigma_k^{-\frac{1}{2}}\mu_k^d\right) = \frac{\Sigma_k^{-\frac{1}{2}}}{2\sqrt{n_k N_d}}\left[2\sum_{i=1}^{N_d}\beta_{ki}(z_i^d y_{ki}) - m_k\sum_{i=1}^{N_d}\beta_{ki}y_{ki}\right], \tag{2.27}$$

where

$$y_{ki} = [z_i^d - \mu_k]^T \Sigma_k^{-1}, \tag{2.28}$$

$$\beta_{ki} = p(k|z_i^d) - (p(k|z_i^d))^2. \tag{2.29}$$

And for the case when $m \neq k$ we get

$$\frac{\partial}{\partial \mu_k}\left(\sqrt{\pi_m^d}\Sigma_m^{-\frac{1}{2}}\mu_m^d\right) = \frac{\Sigma_m^{-\frac{1}{2}}}{2\sqrt{n_m N_d}}\left[m_m\sum_{i=1}^{N_d}\delta_{mki}y_{ki} - 2\sum_{i=1}^{N_d}\delta_{mki}(z_i^d y_{ki})\right], \tag{2.30}$$

where

$$y_{ki} = [z_i^d - \mu_k]^T \Sigma_k^{-1},$$

$$\delta_{mki} = p(k|z_i^d)p(m|z_i^d). \tag{2.31}$$

Equations 2.27 and 2.30 represents a $p \times p$ matrix. These equations are then used to construct $\frac{\partial \Psi^d}{\partial \mu_k}$ in Eq. 2.26. Since the number of Gaussians in the GMM is K, this gives rise to a $Kp \times p$ matrix, which is then used to compute $\frac{\partial L}{\partial \mu_k}$ in Eq. 2.24. Afterwards, stochastic gradient descent is used to modify the UBM to give better discrimination properties:

$$\mu_k^{(t+1)} = \mu_k^{(t)} - \lambda^{(t)}\left(\frac{\partial L^d}{\partial \mu_k}\right)^T, \tag{2.32}$$

where

$$\frac{\partial L^d}{\partial \mu_k} = A\frac{-c^d}{1+\exp[c^d w^T \Psi^d]} w^T \frac{\partial \Psi^d}{\partial \mu_k}, \tag{2.33}$$

$$\lambda^{(t)} = \frac{\lambda^{(t_0)}}{\sqrt{n/D+1}}.$$

This framework can also be easily extended to multi-class cases as in Section 2.4.2. The new discriminative GMM with updated means are then used for SVE, which is then used for training and testing. For further details, please refer to [Tariq *et al.* (2014)] and its supplemental material.

[3]Please refer to the [Tariq (2013)] and [Tariq *et al.* (2014)] for detailed derivation.

2.5 Databases

In the following we describe the databases we use in our experiments in Section 2.6.

2.5.1 *Binghamton University 3D Facial Expression (BU-3DFE) Database*

This is the publicly available BU-3DFE database [Yin *et al.* (2006)]. It is designed to sample facial behaviors in 3D with various prototypical emotional states. It has 3D face scan of a 100 subjects, each performing 6 expressions at 4 intensity levels. It also has the associated texture images. The facial expressions presented in this database include; Anger (AN), Disgust (DI), Fear (FE), Happy (HA), Sad (SA) and Surprise (SU). Each subject also has a neutral face scan. Thus, there are a total of 2500 3D faces scans in this database. Out of the 100 subjects, 56 are females while 44 are males. This dataset is quite diverse and contains subjects with various racial ancestries. Interested readers are referred to [Yin *et al.* (2006)] for further details.

We used an openGL based tool to render multiple views. We generated views with seven pan angles ($0°$, $\pm15°$, $\pm30°$, $\pm45°$) and five tilt angles ($0°$, $\pm15°$, $\pm30°$). These views were generated for each subject with 6 expressions and for the maximum intensity level. This resulted into an image dataset with $5 \times 7 \times \times 6 \times 1 \times 100 = 21000$ images. We used the strongest expression intensity level (21,000 images) to compare our results with some prior works.

Some sample images of a subject with various expressions and intensity levels are shown in Figure 2.1. Similarly, some images of the subject in various pan and tilt angles are shown in Figure 2.2.

2.5.2 *CMU Multi-PIE*

The CMU Multi-PIE database [Gross *et al.* (2010)] is used in the experiments to validate the SSE algorithm developed in Section 2.4.3. We select a subset of the Multi-PIE database and label them for expressions. We use images from 299 subjects from the first three sessions. We select 5 camera views (04_1, 05_0, 05_1, 13_0 and 14_0) and use all of the 19 illumination conditions. Thus, we use approximately 152,000 images in total. We have four expression categories: neutral, positive (smile), negative (squint, disgust) and surprise. We have approximately 59,000 images labeled for neutral,

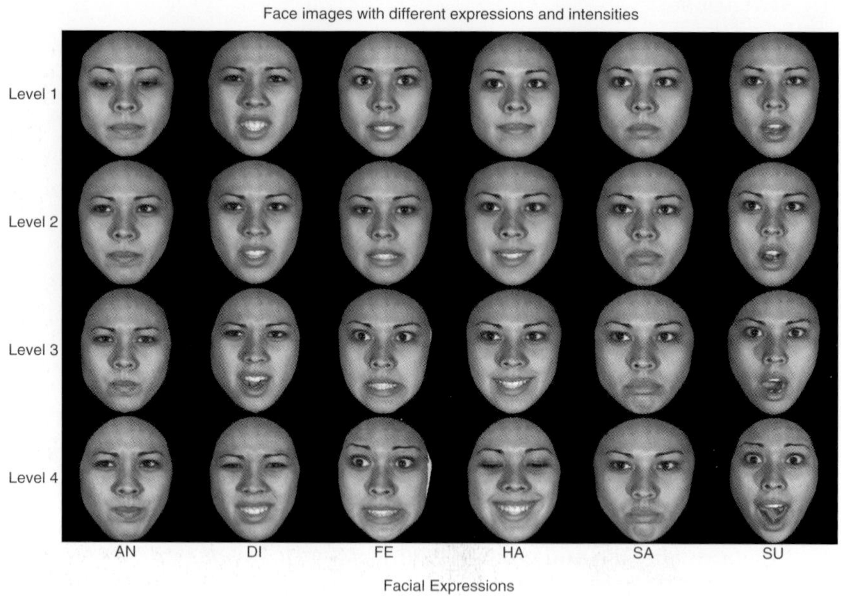

Fig. 2.1: Rendered facial images of a subject with various expressions and intensity levels. The intensity levels are labeled from '1' to '4' with '4' being the most intense.

34,000 for negative, 39,000 for positive and 20,000 for surprise expression. Some example images from CMU Multi-PIE are shown in Figure 2.3.

2.6 Experiments and Discussion

SSVQ and SSE developed in Section 2.4 are then applied for facial expression recognition in [Tariq (2013)], [Tariq *et al.* (2013)] and [Tariq *et al.* (2014)]. Both of these methods are evaluated on the BU-3DFE database outlined in Section 2.5.1, while SSE is further evaluated on CMU-Multi-PIE as well, which is outlined in Section 2.5.2.

For the experiments on the BU-3DFE database we do 5-fold subject independent cross validation on multi-view faces with 7 pan angles and 5 tilt angles with the strongest expression intensity (21,000 images in total). In each fold, around 80% of the images are used for training and 20% for

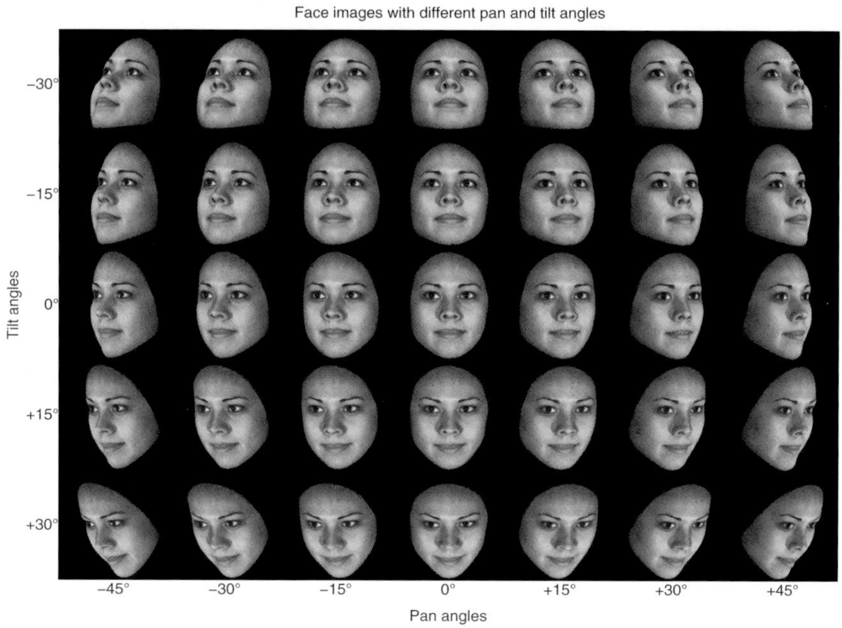

Fig. 2.2: Rendered facial images of a subject with various pan and tilt angles.

validation. The subjects in the training set do not appear in the validation set. Such an experimental setting is chosen to compare the results with prior works of [Zheng *et al.* (2010)] and [Tang *et al.* (2010)].

The images are scaled down to keep computation in check. We then extract features on a dense sampling grid with fixed scale (16×16 pixels) and orientation ($0°$). The initial GMMs are also learned in a fold-independent setting, in the traditional unsupervised manner, using the Expectation Maximization algorithm. The GMM for each fold has 1024 mixtures for SSVQ whereas we use 64 mixtures for SSE. The initial learning rate λ was set to be a small value in stochastic learning. The supervised GMM parameter updates are only for the means of the Gaussian mixtures, although the covariance matrices can also be updated in principle.

Figure 2.4 shows objective function value (Eq. 2.13) for the case of SSVQ decreases, averaged for the expression classes, with supervised iterations for each of the folds. The last figure also shows the average of the five training folds. One can notice that the objective value, in general, re-

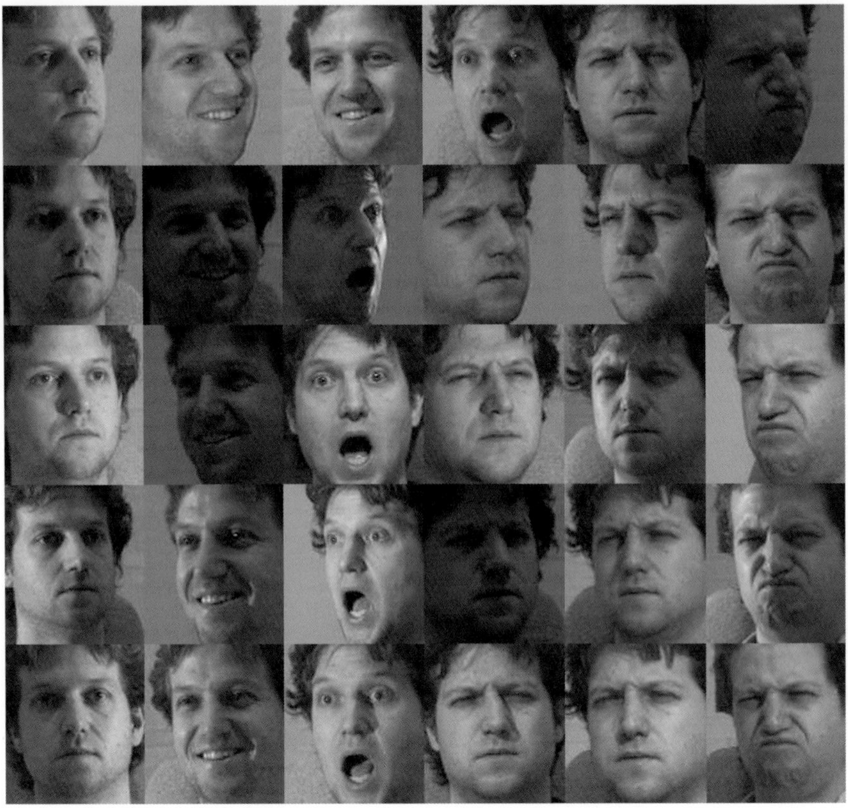

Fig. 2.3: Example images from CMU Multi-PIE database.

duces for all the cases. Similarly figure 2.5 shows the effect of supervised iterations with SSE on the training data in BU-3DFE database.

Table 2.1 shows how the performance increases with supervised training along with comparisons with other works in the same experimental setting.

As shown, the supervised training with SSVQ not only reduces the objective function value on all the folds (Figure 2.4) but also gives a significant increase in testing classification rate of 6.5% with 12 iterations compared with SVQ (Table 2.1). The supervised training with SSE also reduces the objective function value on most of the folds (Figure 2.5) in our experiments with the BU-3DFE database. For one of the folds, the objective function first increases and then decreases afterwards (signaling thereby that the initial learning rate might be a bit high). However, when it comes

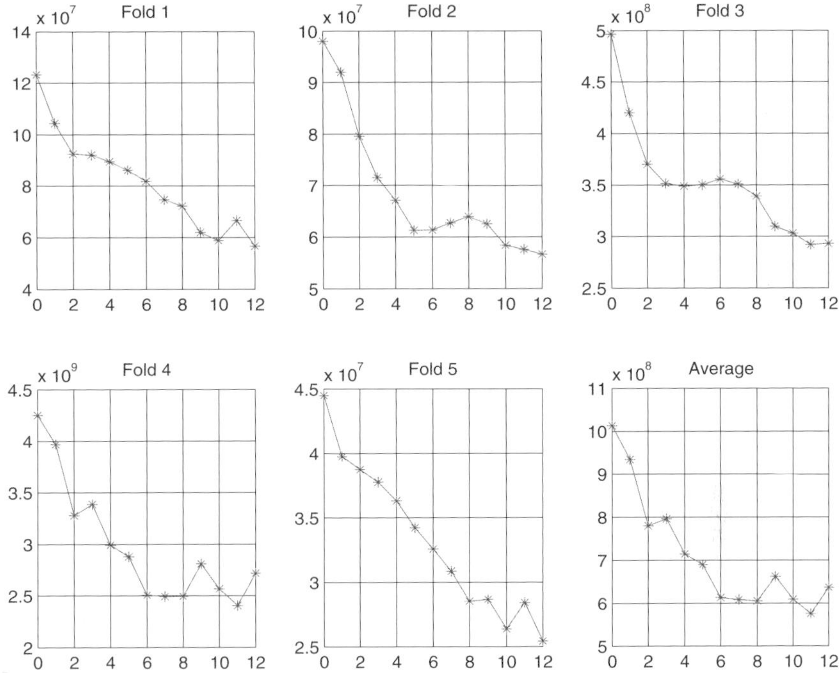

Fig. 2.4: Decrease in objective function value with the supervised iterations (SSVQ) for each of the training folds and average for for the BU-3DFE database. The horizontal axis represents the number of iterations while the vertical axis represents the objective function value.

to the testing classification rate, it gives an improvement of 1.2%. We also compare it with other results in Table 2.1.

One thing to note is that the work by Zheng *et al.* [Zheng *et al.* (2010)] does not include any implicit spatial information. Thus it will be fair to compare it to SSVQ and SSE without using any location information. However, Tang *et al.* [Tang *et al.* (2010)] operate on sequences of patches from the images: thus it can be argued that while doing that, they encode implicit location information. Thus, for a fair comparison we need to compare it with SSVQ+SPM and SSE+SPM. As shown in Table 2.1, in both the comparisons, the supervised training works better. Also note that, in case of SSVQ we use 1024 mixtures while the result with SSE is just with 64 mixtures.

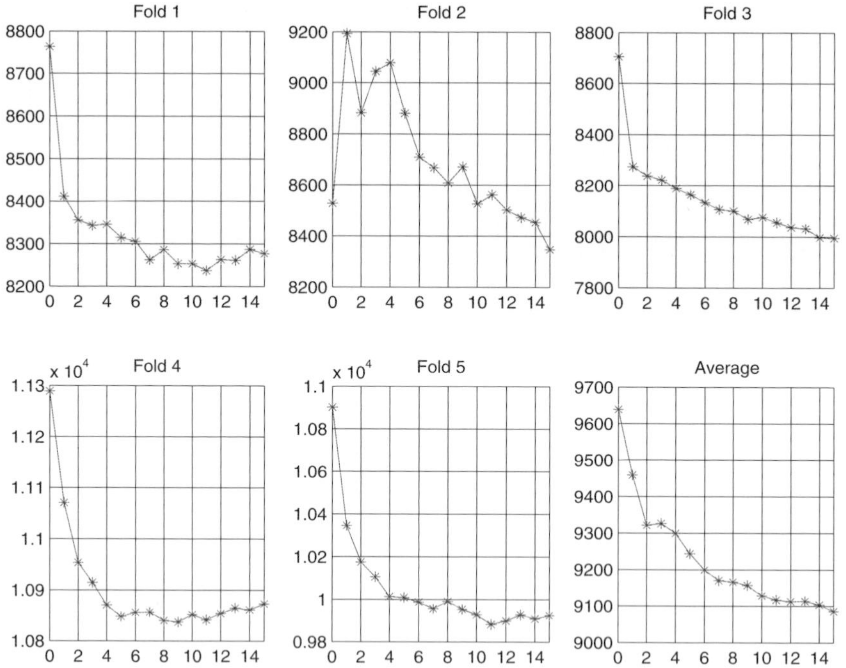

Fig. 2.5: Effect on objective function value with the supervised iterations for each of the training folds and average for the BU-3DFE database for SSE. The horizontal axis represents the number of iterations while the vertical axis represents the objective function value.

It seems from Table 2.1 that the supervised training of the SVE features did not help a lot when compared with the performance without supervised training. It seems SVE features are powerful enough even without any supervised training for this problem. This hypothesis is validated when we look into the training classification rate of all the folds and find that it is very high; almost 100%. The hope of any improvement with supervised training seems to decrease when there are no miss-classified samples in the training data. This is why the decrease in objective function value relative to the initial value is not much; as shown in Figure 2.5, it is between 2% and 9% with a median value of 5.6%.

Thus, we experiment with a more challenging data-set with much greater number of samples and more variation (i.e. CMU Multi-PIE). We experiment with 64, 128 and 256 mixtures and do 6 supervised iterations.

Table 2.1: Comparison in terms of classification rate (for the BU-3DFE database).

Zheng *et al.* [Zheng *et al.* (2010)]	68.2%
Tang *et al.* [Tang *et al.* (2010)]	75.3%
SVQ [Tariq *et al.* (2013)]	63.28%
SSVQ [Tariq *et al.* (2013)]	**69.81%**
SVE [Zhou *et al.* (2009)]	67.8%
SSE [Tariq *et al.* (2014)]	**69.0%**
SSVQ + SPM [Tariq *et al.* (2013)]	**76.16%**
SSE + SPM [Tariq *et al.* (2014)]	**76.6%**

Table 2.2: Performance comparison in terms of percentage classification rate of HG and SHG on Multi-PIE database.

Nmix	64		128		256	
	HG	**SHG**	HG	**SHG**	HG	**SHG**
Trial 1	70.9%	**75.4%**	74.0%	**78.4%**	76.5%	**80.5%**
Trial 2	72.1%	**77.7%**	75.3%	**80.4%**	78.3%	**82.4%**
Trial 3	72.2%	**77.6%**	75.4%	**80.5%**	78.1%	**82.7%**
Average	71.7%	**76.9%**	74.9%	**79.7%**	77.6%	**81.8%**

We use images with 5 camera views, 19 lighting conditions and 299 subjects. We have four expression categories and about 152,000 images in our selected subset. The database is further explained in Section 2.5.2. We divide the images in three subject-independent partitions and use one for training, the other for validation and the third for testing. We experiment with 64, 128 and 256 mixtures. We repeat the experiments three times with randomizing the partitions.

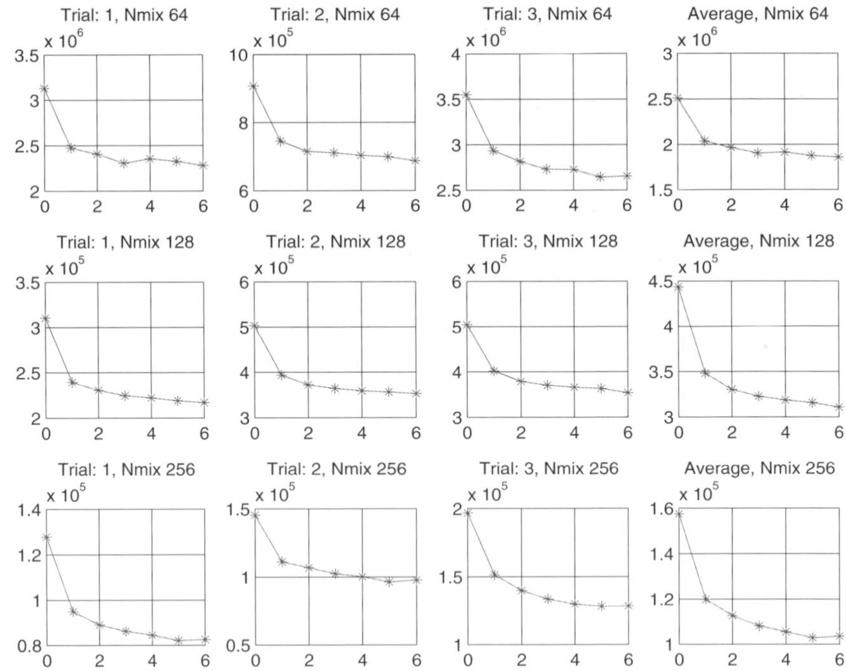

Fig. 2.6: Effect on objective function value with supervised iterations for each of the trials for different number of mixtures and averages for Multi-PIE database. The horizontal axis represents the number of iterations while the vertical axis represents the objective function value.

We show the results for the effect of supervised training on the objective function value in Figure 2.6, and that on training classification rate in Figure 2.7 for different numbers of mixtures in the GMM, three trials and their averages. Figure 2.6 shows that the supervised training reduces the objective function significantly for all the cases. This reduction is from 24% to 35% of the initial objective function value, with a median value of 29.9%. This is indeed significant. When we compare it to Figure 2.7, we find that the training classification rate also increases significantly in all the cases. This also translates into significant increase in testing classification rate as shown in Table 2.2. The performance improvement is anywhere between 4.0 % and 5.6%.

One very significant result from Table 2.2 is that we can get better classification rate with using half the number of mixtures in UBM with

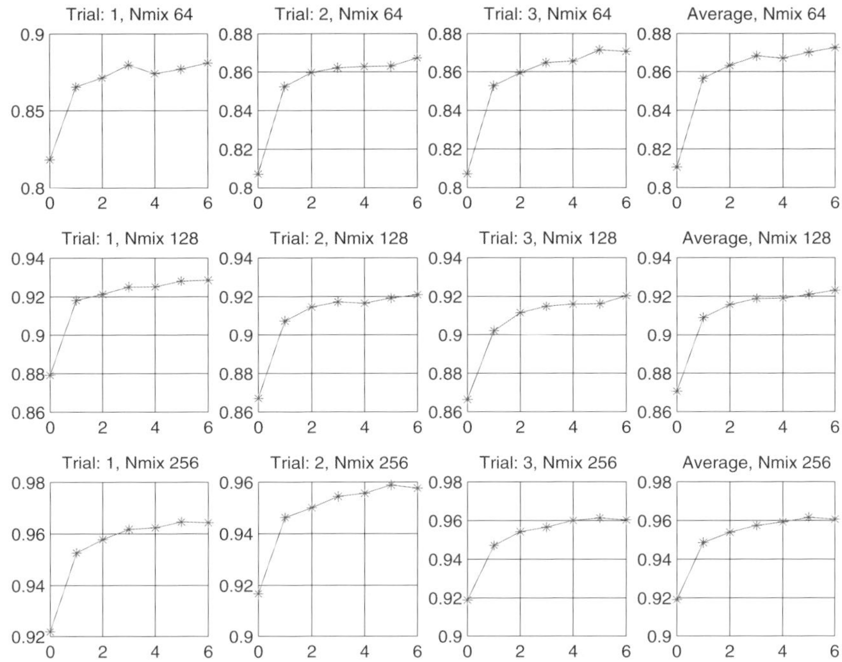

Fig. 2.7: Effect on training classification rate with supervised iterations for each of the trials for different number of mixtures and averages for Multi-PIE database. The horizontal axis represents the number of iterations while the vertical axis represents the classification rate.

doing just a few supervised iterations. This results in reducing the testing time by half. One more thing to note from Figures 2.6 and 2.7 is that more significant improvement with supervised training on the Multi-PIE data-set happens in the first few iterations. Afterwards the performance improvement is incremental.

2.7 Concluding Remarks

Inspired by the very successful Bag-of-Words and SVE framework for image categorization, we presented novel task-specific supervised algorithms for discriminative training of GMMs and their application to facial expression recognition. The algorithms demonstrates significant performance gain compared with their unsupervised counterparts on the BU3DFE and Multi-PIE datasets. In future work we can explore supervised training for full GMM parameters (mean, mixture weights, and covariance matrices) with proper regularization.

The framework is general and can easily be applied to other classification tasks as well, such as object recognition, face recognition, speaker identification, and audio event recognition. Specifically, the method will be integrated into a student monitoring system for use in distance learning. This application will be presented in Chapter 7.

Chapter 3

3D Face Modeling

3.1 Introduction

Traditional facial image processing techniques based their analysis on 2D models such as intensity images in various color space or frequency domain such as Fourier and wavelet transforms. However, the variations in pose, illumination and expression (PIE) of the images create immense difficulties in 2D signal based face processing. The two main solutions for these challenges are compensating the 2D variation compensation and modeling 3D face shape and texture. The former approach compensates for the environmental factors by learning appearance models such as efficient lighting model [Rara *et al.* (2008)], pose adaptive face recognition [Cao *et al.* (2010)], and compressive sensing [Nagesh and Li (2009)]. However, these compensation methods can usually lead to overfitting or probabilistic instability and therefore are applicable to only small number of restricted cases. Because of this, in recent years, more and more effort is being put into the second approach of using 3D models of faces. For general arbitrary configurations of PIE conditions, the 3D model based approaches show more potential for attacking the nature of the problem and are therefore more robust to broader ranges of environment configurations.

In another aspect, the recent facial signal modeling techniques fall into the two main groups of *appearance based* and *feature based*. The appearance based techniques model the facial appearance holistically; they treat the whole face region as a pattern, ignoring the spatial information of detailed facial features. The most important appearance based methods include Eigenfaces [Turk and Pentland (1991)], Fisherfaces [Belhumeur *et al.* (1997)], Active Appearance model (AAM) [Cootes *et al.* (2001)], 3D-AAM [Mitchell *et al.* (2002)], and 3D morphable model (3DMM)

[Blanz and Vetter (1999)]. Naturally, the appearance based methods model the dense details of the face into a feature supervector. Therefore they are able to reconstruct highly accurate details of facial geometry and texture. However, these methods usually work on a very high dimensional space with highly nonconvex cost function, therefore they are computationally complex and vulnerable to local minimum and low convergence rate. On the other hand, feature-based approaches rely upon the localization of facial features. The approaches of this category require or involve a step where the facial features, such as corners and contours of the eyes, nose, and mouth, are accurately localized. Early methods such as Active shape model (ASM) [Cootes *et al.* (1995)] use the features extracted from 2D images. Later methods expand the feature based paradigm to 3D data such as [Wang *et al.* (2006); Hu *et al.* (2004b)]. Unlike appearance based techniques, feature based methods have important advantages of efficiency and high tolerance; moreover, with recent advances in graphics and the development of hybrid models, the accuracy of feature based facial modeling is catching up with that of appearance based methods.

In this chapter, we introduce a framework for feature based 3D face processing with the connection to the applications in distance learning and other fields. For 3D model acquisition and tracking, we introduce a novel noninvasive, reliable, fully automatic algorithm for reconstructing 3D facial model and tracking nonrigid motion using a single low resolution 2D camera and commodity RGB-D cameras. The fitting algorithms are based on an efficient iterative optimization procedure with linearized cost functions. The motion model is compatible with MPEG-4 facial animation standard. The algorithms have been implemented into practical demonstrations which provide real-time performance on laptop computers. Experiments with the public data show high quantitative performances and realistic visual results.

The following sections are organized as follows: The 3D reconstruction algorithms for single or couple of 2D images are described in Section 3.2. In Section 3.3, a 3D nonrigid tracking algorithm is examined. Section 3.4 introduces the adapted algorithms and system for face modeling from RGB-D images. Finally, Section 3.5 will summarize the chapter and propose several directions for future work.

3.2 3D Face Model Reconstruction from 2D Images

3D face reconstruction from 2D images is an important problem in computer vision. In the past few decades, many approaches have been proposed including 3D from stereopsis [Furukawa and Ponce (2009)], 3D morphable model based methods [Romdhani and Vetter (2003)], structure from motion [Tomasi and Kanade (1992)] and shape from shading techniques [Zhang *et al.* (1999)].

Among these, 3D morphable model (3DMM) based algorithms have attracted more and more attention in recent years. Vetter *et al.* [Romdhani and Vetter (2003)] proposed a family of 3D fitting algorithms to recover the facial shape and texture parameters of the 3DMM from the appearance features. Although being able to give accurate shape and controllable texture models, these methods tend to extract complicated high dimensional features and introduce very big optimization problems. Therefore, they are usually very slow to fit a face, which is not suitable for most applications in reality.

To speed up the fitting process, Hu *et al.* [Hu *et al.* (2004b)] proposed a fully automatic linear algorithm to recover the shape information according to sparsely corresponded 2D facial feature points. The 3D face geometry was recovered from a frontal view input face image and then the texture was extracted from the input image directly. Being a state-of-the-art method for fitting 3DMM to sparse features, the algorithm works very efficiently and gives reasonable reconstruction results. The main restriction of this work is that it requires the input to be a frontal face image. This requirement is hard to satisfy when the face image is captured passively. In addition, the texture mapped from a single image cannot cover the whole face model and thus there will be holes after mapping the texture to the reconstructed 3D face shape.

Following the sparse feature fitting algorithm in [Hu *et al.* (2004b)], this chapter introduces two new methods for 3D face reconstruction from a single image of arbitrary view and from a pair of stereo images. Powered by morphable model and iterative optimization techniques, our methods can preserve the substantial advantages and overcome the restrictions of the old method. We also recover the facial texture by mapping and merging from the input images to provide the complete and photorealistic 3D face model.

3.2.1 *Related Work*

Along the line of fitting 3DMM to sparse features, [Zhang *et al.* (2006)] recovered the shape from one single frontal face image. After that, the images of other views were used to refine the shape estimation and supplement the texture using minimum variance estimation. Although the other views may help improve the shape model, the quality of the estimated shape is principally determined by the first fitting with the frontal face image.

In another work, [Park and Jain (2006)] introduced an approach closely related to the framework proposed in this chapter. From two frames of a video, one of which is frontal, a sparse set of 3D points is reconstructed and then fitted it to a generic model using thin plate splines. Our method is significantly different from this method as in our work, at the dense fitting step, instead of being interpolated by a generic model, the morphable model is searched in a linear space learned from training faces. In this way, the new shape is constrained to be a combination of known real faces and is therefore not only accurately matched but also more likely to be a regular human face shape. Besides, by using both images as texture sources, in our new approach, the restriction of including a frontal image is relaxed and the face textures will be more complete.

While the facial texture can be directly extracted from the images, the albedo of the facial surface is harder to retrieve. In the recent works of [Taheri *et al.* (2013)] and [Biswas *et al.* (2009)], the albedo of the face is estimated jointly with face pose from a sequence of video frames using the Rao-Blackwellized particle filters.

These advances in the field suggested the direction of jointly estimation of multiple aspects shape, pose, and texture to make the reconstruction more robust to environment condition. Our methods that will be introduced in this chapter are strongly inspired and influenced by this direction.

3.2.2 *3D Reconstruction from a Single Image of Arbitrary View*

A neutral face model of a specific person is represented by a shape vector S consisting the stacked 3D coordinates of N vertices defined on a correspondence reference frame.

$$S = (X_1, Y_1, Z_1, X_2, Y_2, Z_2, \ldots, X_N, Y_N, Z_N)^T. \tag{3.1}$$

Following the traditional 3D morphable model [Blanz and Vetter (1999)], we project the facial shape vector onto the linear space spanned by PCA basis vectors learnt from a training set of 3D faces:

$$S = \bar{S} + P\vec{\sigma}, \tag{3.2}$$

where P and σ are the PCA basis and coefficients respectively.

When projected to 2D image space, the projection of the vertices of S are given by:

$$S'' = M(RS + t), \tag{3.3}$$

where M is camera projection matrix, R is rotation matrix and t is translation vector.

In the analysis by synthesis [Blanz and Vetter (2003)] framework, the cost functions of the initial fitting and the motion model fitting are

$$C_{fitting}(\sigma, c, R, t) = ||S^* - c(R(\bar{S} + P\vec{\sigma})) + t)||_2, \tag{3.4}$$

where S^* is the 2D target landmark points.

To improve the efficiency, our algorithms search for parameters in a subspace of m 2D landmark points of S'. Resampling the shapes from Eqs. 3.2 and 3.3, we have these formulas for the subvectors:

$$s' = \bar{s} + p\vec{\sigma}, \tag{3.5}$$

$$s'' = M(Rs' + t), \tag{3.6}$$

where $\bar{s}$, s', s'', p, f are the subvectors of $\bar{S}$, S', S'', P respectively.

The cost function in the subspace can be written as

$$c_{fitting}(\sigma, c, R, t) = ||s^* - c(R(\bar{s} + p\vec{\sigma})) + t)||_2, \tag{3.7}$$

where s^* is the 2D target landmark points.

These cost functions are highly nonconvex and nonlinear and therefore normally require nonlinear time to solve.

Based on this model, we introduce our *Iterative Linearized Optimization* procedure which reduces the complexity of the problem posed in Eq. 3.7 into linear time. Our optimization algorithm relies on an iterative procedure. At each iteration, the following three steps are performed:

Step 1 In the first step of an iteration, the translation vector t is optimized. From Eq. 3.6 we have the optimized translation vector to be:

$$t = M^{-1}(s'' - M(R(s')). \tag{3.8}$$

Step 2 In this step, the rotation R and projection M are optimized. Both of the rotation matrix and perspective projection are highly nonlinear and nonconvex. In the following, we will make the assumptions that lead to the linear approximation of them.

For M, we assume that the camera is orthographic, hence, the camera matrix M reduced to a single scale factor c.

For R, we will separate the three pose angles α, β, γ and solve them together with c in three different substeps. At the first substep, α and c will be optimized together. In order to linearize Eq. 3.6, we substitute α and c by two new arguments $x = c \times \cos(\alpha)$ and $y = c \times \sin(\alpha)$. With this substitution, Eq. 3.6 will become a linear system of x and y which is solved by linear least square. α and c are then recovered by $\alpha = \arctan(y/x)$ and $c = \sqrt{x^2 + y^2}$. Similar operations are applied to find β and γ through substitution variables.

Step 3 At this step, the shape coefficient σ are found by solving Eq. 3.5 by constrained linear least squares with the constraints to be $\alpha \leq r$ where r is some constant threshold vector. These inequality constraints emerge as the restrictions to keep the new face to have regular human face shape.

In order to find a suitable threshold r, we employ a commonly used assumption that the facial shape has normal priors with a probability density function of: $p(\alpha) \sim e^{\frac{1}{2}\sum_i \frac{\alpha_i^2}{\sigma_i^2}}$. This leads us to the choice for constraint thresholds proportional to the standard deviation of the representation of the training data in the principal component space: $r_i = \lambda\sigma_i$ (λ is a constant). Our experiments show that this choice for threshold gives better results than using the eigenvalues as in [Hu *et al.* (2004b)]. Solving Eq. 3.5 with these constraints, the shape principal coefficients is recovered by

$$\sigma = (p^T p + \lambda \operatorname{diag}(r^2)^{-1})^{-1} p^T (s' - \bar{s}). \tag{3.9}$$

After initialization, the three steps are alternatively repeated until convergence. In our experiments, the process normally converges in less than ten rounds.

3.2.3 *3D Reconstruction from Stereo Images*

In this section, we apply the face shape model formulated in Section 3.2.2 for a fitting algorithm of stereo images captured from calibrated cameras. Our reconstruction algorithm works in a coarse-to-fine fashion. First, from a collection of salient points located on two input face images, a sparse set of corresponding 3D points is reconstructed. After that, these reconstructed 3D points will be used to build a dense 3DMM model of the facial shape. Finally, the texture from both input images will be mapped and merged

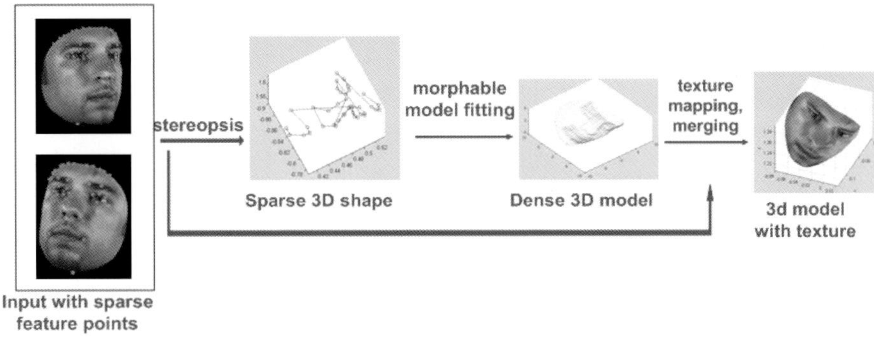

Fig. 3.1: Coarse-to-fine 3D face reconstruction framework.

altogether on the reference frame of the 3DMM. The entire process will generate a detailed, textured 3D face model. The framework for our method is depicted in Figure 3.1.

3D sparse shape reconstruction To reconstruct a sparse set of 3D feature points, we first need to locate enough facial feature points and find their correspondences on the two input images. This can be done automatically using a face alignment algorithm such as the one in [Cristinacce *et al.* (2004)]. In this section, because we do not concentrate on solving this problem, we use the prior information about the location of feature points instead of locating them directly. With the corresponding feature points on the two calibrated images, the 3D feature points are reconstructed by triangulation.

3D dense shape model fitting In this step, we fit the sparse set of reconstructed 3D points to 3DMM. We reuse the face model used in the algorithm in Section 3.2.2. However, instead of having the input of 2D feature points, we now have a set of 3D feature points, which allow faster and more accurate fitting algorithm.

Considering Eqs. 3.5 and 3.6 but with $\bar{s}$, s', s'', p, f are the 3D subvectors, the iterative procedure is updated with the following steps:

Initialization: assign $\bar{s}$ to s'

Step 1: Apply the Procrustes analysis to solve Eq. 3.6. In this step, the R, c, and t that would fit s' and s'' the best are found. In our algorithm, we use the method of finding the eigenvector of the correlation matrix corresponding to the least eigenvalue for the Procrustes analysis.

Step 2: Similar to the 2D case, σ is found by solving Eq. 3.5 as a

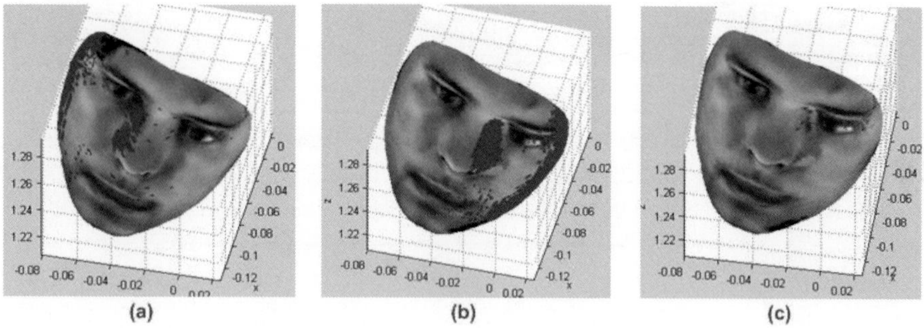

Fig. 3.2: Texture mapping and merging: (a), (b): texture mapped from two images (c): combined texture. The blue areas indicate the locations where texture is missing.

constrained linear least-squares problem.

After initialization, Step 1 and Step 2 are alternatively repeated in each iteration. In our experiments, the process converges in at most ten rounds.

Texture mapping The texture of the model's vertices are mapped from the images by using the camera model recovered in the fitting step. For frontal images, we have most of the texture needed because almost all of the vertices are available. For non-frontal images, more parts of the face are occluded and the their textures are not available at the input image. For those cases, we make the assumption that the texture of the face is symmetric and therefore we can use the texture of the corresponding point in the opposite side if they are available.

In the texture recovering step, the recovered shape is projected onto both input images to find texture coordinates of model's vertices. At each view point, a depth buffer is used to check the visibility of the vertices of the face, only the visible ones are textured by inverse mapping. In the areas of the face where two extracted textures are overlapped, the color of a vertex will be the average of two texture values. Figure 3.2 illustrates the texture obtained from two images and the merged texture.

3.2.4 *Experiments and Evaluation*

3.2.4.1 *Experiment Setups*

In order to demonstrate the effectiveness and evaluate the accuracy of the 3D face model fitting algorithms, efficient methods for measuring perfor-

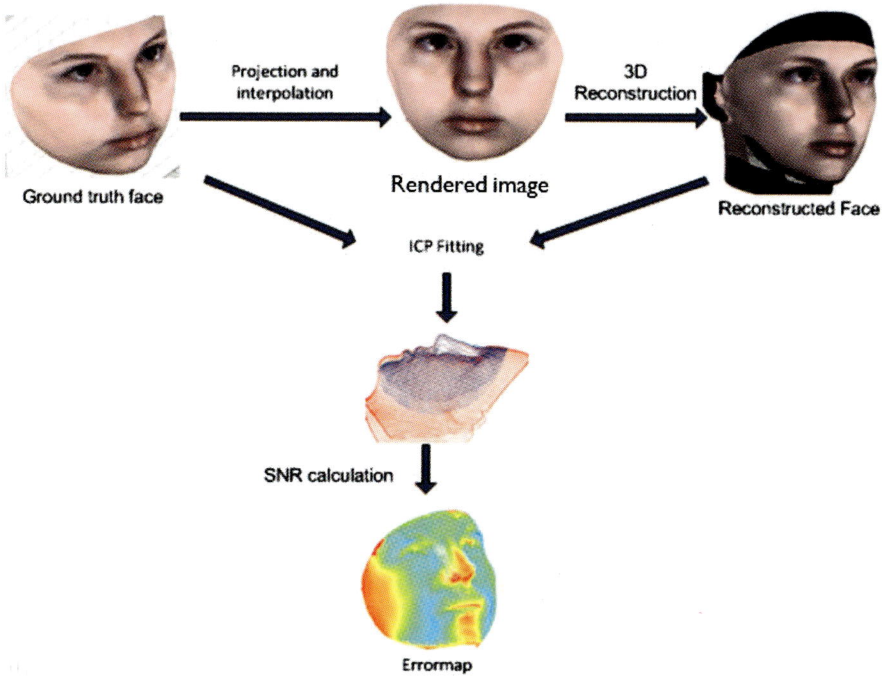

Fig. 3.3: Framework of quantitative evaluation algorithm.

mance of the algorithms are essentially desired. The currently available evaluation methods are either based on subjective experiments or indirect evaluation on face recognition [Hu *et al.* (2004a); Romdhani *et al.* (2002)]; i.e., there is no information about the shape/texture error provided, which made it difficult to further analyze the reconstruction algorithm and improve the features they used. An effective quantitative evaluation is required to give us the clues for finding the strength of the algorithms, investigating their weakness and suggesting further guidance for feature selection and algorithm refinement. In this section, we proposed to use signal-noise ratio (SNR) and error maps (EM) to quantitatively evaluate the accuracy of a 3D face reconstruction algorithm and provide its detail performance on shape recovery.

The framework of our quantitative evaluation method is described in Figure 3.3. From the ground truth 3D face database [Hu *et al.* (2007)], we obtain the input 2D face image by projecting a 3D face onto 2D plane.

This 2D face image and the extracted features will then be fed to the evaluated reconstruction system to get the reconstructed 3D face. To compare the ground truth 3D face shape and the reconstructed 3D face, they are first aligned to each other by *iterative closest point* (ICP) algorithm. The difference returned from the fitting process will then be used as the error term for calculating SNR. These measurements on all the vertices will congregate to form the error map, which provides the final detailed result of the evaluation process.

3.2.4.2 *Single Image Fitting*

In this section, the performance of three algorithms Inverse Compositional Image Alignment (ICIA) [Romdhani and Vetter (2003)], Sparse 3DMM [Jiang *et al.* (2005)] and ours are compared. ICIA is a state-of-the-art method based on a detailed appearance based model of shape and texture. The algorithm finds the 3D model configuration by minimizing the error made when the model is inversely projected back to the image domain. Sparse 3DMM is another state-of-the-art algorithm using sparse feature points to fit 3DMM of facial shape on frontal images.

We follow the procedure for quantitative evaluation of 3D reconstruction algorithms proposed in the previous section. Specifically, we train the three algorithms on USF 3D database [Blanz and Vetter (1999)]. The testing is done on 135 faces of IFP 3D dataset [Hu *et al.* (2007)].

To concentrate on comparing performance of fitting algorithm without the effect of quality of feature point detection, in this experiment, we use landmark ground-truths which are previously hand labeled.

The comparison of accuracy by RMSE and SNRDB over pan angles is shown in Figures 3.4 and 3.5

From the quantitative evaluation, we can conclude that the performance of our algorithm on nonfrontal images surpasses the other two methods. Our performance is also affected very little by the change in pan angles.

3.2.4.3 *Stereo Images Fitting*

Figure 3.6 illustrates the reconstruction results of our algorithm on the corresponding samples on Figure 3.7. Subjectively assessing, the face shapes and textures are accurately reconstructed. The texture is reconstructed almost completely, which covers both the frontal and side areas of the face without holes and gives a realistic looking. Compared with related texture mapping based methods such as [Hu *et al.* (2004b)], our algorithm

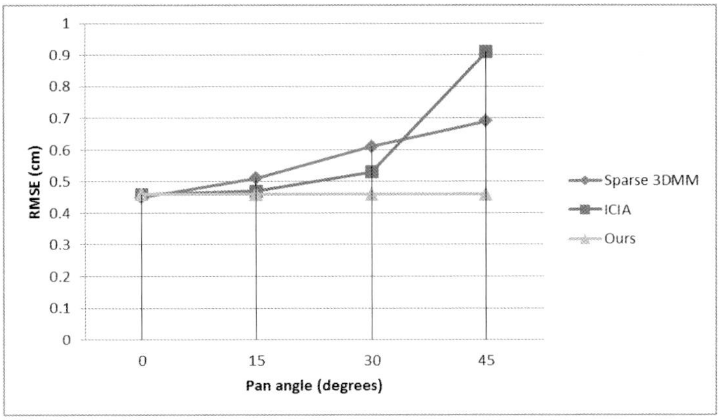

Fig. 3.4: Root mean square error comparison among three fitting methods with four pose angles from 0 to 45 degrees.

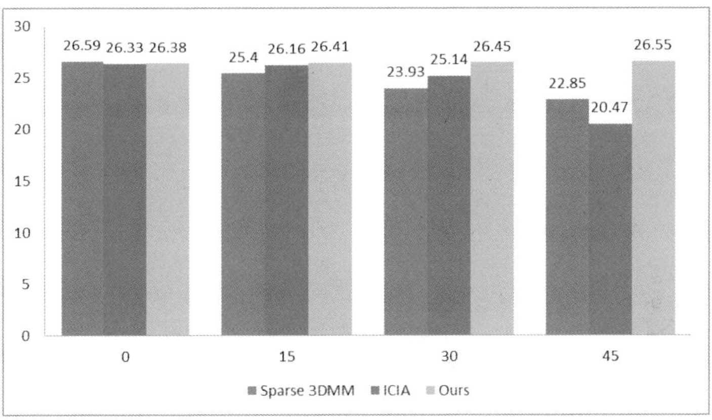

Fig. 3.5: Signal-to-noise ratio (in dB) comparison among three fitting methods with four pose angles from 0 to 45 degrees.

generates more complete face texture due to the use of the texture from all input images, as shown in Figure 3.8.

The accuracy of the reconstruction is also quantitatively evaluated by measuring the disparity between the synthetic shape and the groundtruth shape used to generate input images. We align those couples by Procrustes transformation and measure the distance between the corresponding ver-

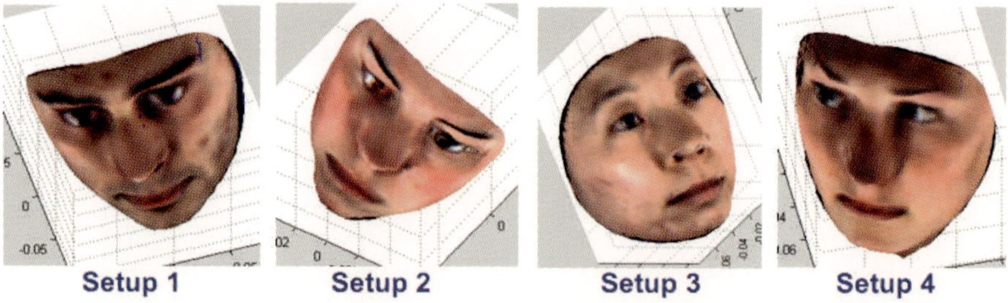

Fig. 3.6: Rendered reconstruction results.

Setups	Image1			Image2		
	Angles (degrees)	Distance (cm)	Sample image	Angles (degrees)	Distance (cm)	Sample image
1: one frontal, one other view	0, 0, 0	150		30, 0, 0	100	
2: two symmetrically non-frontal views	-30, 0, 0	150		30, 0, 0	100	
3: various yaw-pich-roll angles	-20, -10, 10	150		30, 10, 0	120	
4: with an extreme yaw angle	-20, -10, 10	120		60, 0, 0	120	

Fig. 3.7: Setups for image pairs

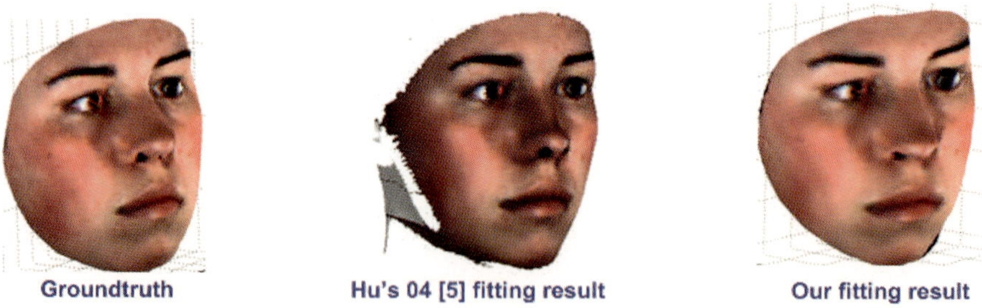

Fig. 3.8: Comparison of fitting results of [Hu *et al.* (2004b)] and our algorithm with groundtruth.

tices. The mean RMS error of all the setups is 2.3 mm. Since most previous 3DMM based algorithms are only evaluated indirectly by recognition accuracy [Phillips *et al.* (2003)], we are not able to compare our algorithm with them. However, the work in [Hu *et al.* (2004b)] has quantitative evaluation

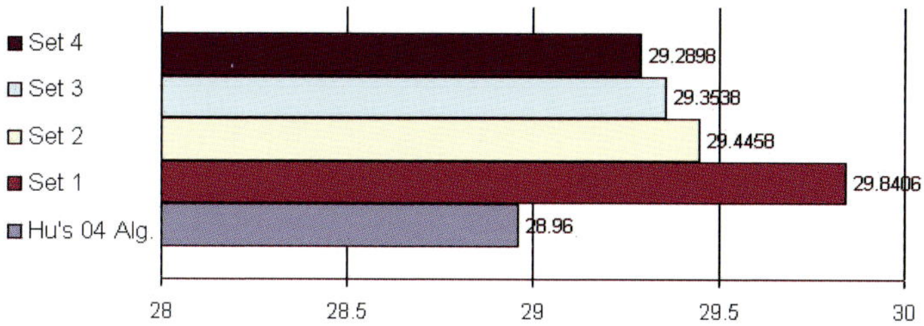

Fig. 3.9: SNRDB of our algorithm on 4 setups and [Hu *et al.* (2004b)].

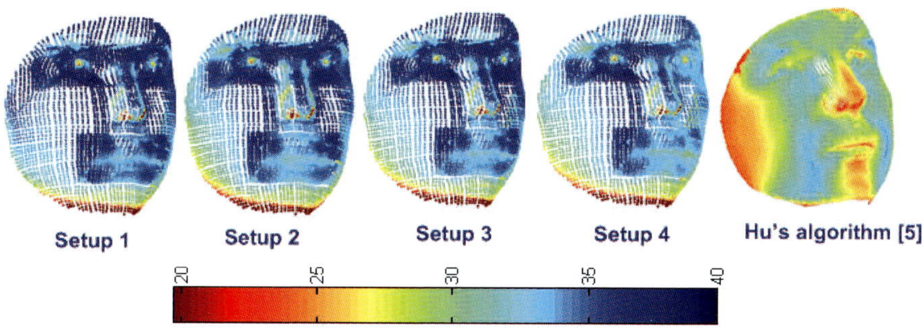

Fig. 3.10: Error map in SNRDB of our algorithm on 4 setups and Hu's algorithm drawn with colormap.

available [Le *et al.* (2009)] in terms of the signal-to-noise ratio (SNR) and errormaps. We will compare our method with this state-of-the-arts work.

The graph of mean SNR measured in db of our algorithm on 4 setups compared with Hu's algorithm is shown in Figure 3.9. The error map for the local SNRDB is depicted in Figure 3.10.

From the SNR graph and error maps, we can see that our method obtains consistently better performance in all of the four test sets. More importantly, the error also decreases significantly in the important areas of the faces. With the proposed resampled correspondence mask, those parts are the most accurately reconstructed.

We implement our algorithm in Matlab and the time used to recover model shape and texture is 5.2 seconds on a 2GHz Core Duo CPU laptop computer. Our speed is comparable to Hu's algorithm [Hu *et al.* (2004b)] and is much faster than dense feature based algorithms [Furukawa and Ponce (2009); Romdhani and Vetter (2003)]. The speeds of the various

Table 3.1: Speed comparison of our algorithm with related works.

Algorithm	Running time	Processor
Vetter's 99 (SNO)	4.5 mins	2.0 GHz
Vetter's 2003 (ICIA)	30 secs	2.8 GHz
Vetter's 2005 (MFF)	70 secs	3.0 GHz
Hu's 04	~5 secs	1.3 GHz
Ponce's 2007	>20 mins	N/A
Our method	5.2 secs	2.0 GHz

algorithms processing the similar input images are compared in Table 3.1.

3.3 3D Face Model Tracking from 2D Videos

3.3.1 *Introduction*

In the previous chapter, we have investigated the techniques for analyzing and reconstructing the 3D structure of human face shapes. While studying the static geometrical features of the human faces provides important cues for understanding identity and characteristics of the subject, analyzing spatio-temporal dynamic data of facial 3D motion through tracking enables richer understanding of the subject's behavior [Lewis and Pighin (2006)] and allows realistic facial animations. With the recent advances of sensing and data analyzing techniques, 3D face motion tracking has been evolving expeditiously and playing a crucial role in multiple important applications such as non-frontal view face recognition, and performance driven avatars [Levine and Yu (2009)].

Most of the current successful methods for 3D motion tracking require lab environment with special equipment such as 3D scanner [Weise *et al.* (2011)], multiple 2D cameras [Beeler *et al.* (2010)] and extraordinary computing power which are not readily available for portable devices. Moreover, the complicated equipment and algorithms make the tracking session less convenient and more invasive.

In this chapter we introduce a novel noninvasive, reliable, fully automatic algorithm for tracking nonrigid motion using a single low resolution 2D camera. Our algorithm concurrently optimizes both rigid and nonrigid facial motions in linear time from a set of visually tracked landmark points.

The nonrigid motions are coded into MPEG 4's facial animation parameters which are used for performance-driven avatar animation. The algorithm is highly efficient and is able to perform in real time on a portable device. The experimental results show that our system achieves more realistic animation than other systems with the same modality.

3.3.2 *Literature Review*

Markerless facial motion capture and retargeting animation have been drawing a lot of attention in recent years. Current successful techniques exploit multiple modalities and modeling paradigms including monocular video [Tang and Huang (Oct. 2008)], multiview camera racks [Beeler *et al.* (2010); Bradley *et al.* (2010)], and from depth images [Weise *et al.* (2011)].

A typical tracking system consists of two main components: Visual tracking and motion model. For visual tracking, traditional optical flow [Shi and Tomasi (1994)] and its variants are widely used for detecting the movement of facial features. Recent robust tracking methods such as SIFT flow [Liu *et al.* (2011)] and SURF [Bay *et al.* (2006)] are also interesting approaches to the problem. However, because of heavy computation, these methods are more suitable for offline analysis. For motion models, the Facial Action Coding System (FACS) is widely used for recognizing and describing the muscular activity of the human face into Action Units (AUs)[Ekman (1993)]. FACS is a reliable, largest and accurate reference to determine the categories of facial behavior and therefore is used by many successful systems such as [Weise *et al.* (2011); McLaughlin *et al.* (2011)]. Another system of modeling facial animation is the MPEG-4 facial animation parameters(FAPs). With the standardized specification and parameters independent from the facial model, the MPEG-4 facial animation standard has been used in a broad range of applications including entertainment, medicine and telecommunication. Some of the notable face tracking and animation works using MPEG-4 are [Tang and Huang (Oct. 2008); Gachery and Magnenat-Thalmann (2001)].

The methods span between the extremes of the fundamental tradeoff between the quality of the model and the efficiency of tracking algorithms. On one end, the high performance systems recover highly detailed models based on 2D appearance features [Beeler *et al.* (2010); Bradley *et al.* (2010)] or 3D geometry from depth camera [Weise *et al.* (2011)]. While providing high quality motion tracking and graphics, these methods utilize powerful hardware setup and complicated algorithms which are not suitable for portable or low power devices.

On the other end, many works based their tracking and fitting on a sparse set of landmark points [Tao and Huang (1999); Tang and Huang (Oct. 2008); Sarris *et al.* (Oct. 2002)]. Although more efficient than the first type, these methods are usually able to recover the general movement of the face but not sensitive enough to capture subtle movement. Also, the tracked models are low-resolution and not suitable for realistic rendering. One of the notable algorithms of this family was first proposed by Tao and Huang [Tao and Huang (1999)] and has been improved by Tu [Tu *et al.* (2007)] and Tang [Tang and Huang (Oct. 2008)]. The real time tracking method is based on the piece-wise Bézier volume (PBVD) to interpolate the 3D NURBS surfaces from a set of control points. These surfaces form a 3D mesh which contains a set of feature points. The 2D correspondences of these feature points are tracked by classic KLT style optical flow. The Bézier volume parameters and geometry are recovered by gradient descent with linearized cost function's gradient. The linearization makes the algorithm run in real time (10 fps) on personal computers. However, the assumptions of close to zero rotation angles used in the gradient linearization make the tracking very unstable in nonfrontal view poses. Moreover, the PBVD free-form surface model cannot model realistic facial expressions which may generate erroneous tracking result.

Our work tries to find the balance of the quality-efficiency trade off by using a hybrid 3D morphable model. The visual tracking is performed on a sparse set of landmark points which assure the efficiency; on the other hand, these landmark points are then fitted into a highly detailed deformation model which will enable high quality motion analysis.

3.3.3 *Real Time 3D Face Tracking from 2D Videos*

In Section 3.2, we have formulated the 3D model of an neutral face by PCA of faces from different subjects. In this section, we will model the displacement between the neutral and expressive models. We employ the MPEG4's facial animation parameters (FAPs) [Ostermann (2002)] to be the basis for deformation. Each parameter of the FAP controls the 3D motion of a set of vertices according to a activation of a group of muscle. The motion vectors are piecewise linear functions of FAP values:

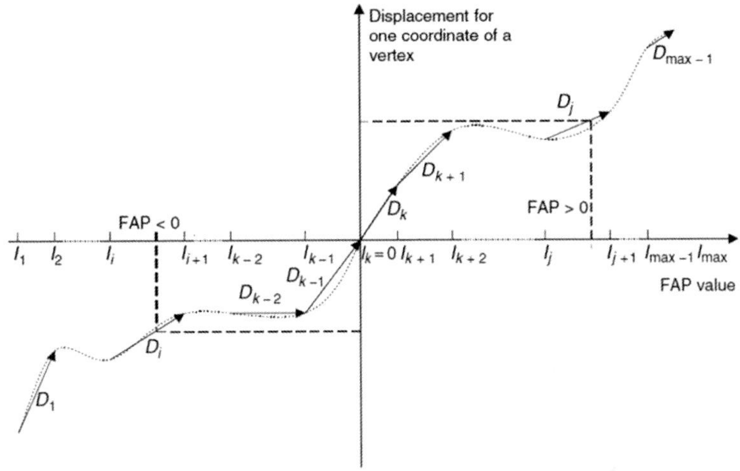

Fig. 3.11: Piecewise linear function of FAP value giving approximation of vertex motion.

$$P'_m = P_m + FAPU * [(I_{k+1} - 0) * D_{m,k} + (I_{k+2} - Ik + 1) * D_{m,k+1} \\ + \cdots (I_j - I_{j-1}) * D_{m,j-1} + (FAP - I_j) * D_{m,j}]. \tag{3.10}$$

Figure 3.11 illustrates an example of these functions. The construction of the motion model will be detailed in Chapter 5 where we design the 3D avatar controlled by the tracking model in this chapter.

The *Facial animation table* (FAT) for the model is constructed by interpolating from manual designed deformation of fiducial points following [Jiang *et al.* (2002)]. In our model, the FAP functions are assumed to be linear to FAP values. Therefore, the displacement from the neutral model is the linear combination of unit displacements:

$$S' = S + F\overrightarrow{\lambda}, \tag{3.11}$$

where S' is the expressive face which is the result of the deformation from the neutral face S; F is the linear FAP basis; and λ are FAP values.

When projected to 2D image space, the projection of the vertices of S' are given by:

$$S'' = M(RS' + t), \tag{3.12}$$

where M is camera projection matrix, R is rotation matrix and t is translation vector.

To improve the efficiency, similar to the algorithm in Section 3.2, our algorithms search for parameters in a subspace of m 2D landmark points of S'. Resampling the shapes from Eqs. 3.2, 3.11, and 3.12, we have these formulas for the subvectors:

$$s = \bar{s} + p\overrightarrow{\alpha}, \tag{3.13}$$

$$s' = s + f\overrightarrow{\lambda}, \tag{3.14}$$

$$s'' = M(Rs' + t), \tag{3.15}$$

where $\bar{s}$, s, s', s'',p, f are the subvectors of $\bar{S}$, S, S', S'',P respectively.

In the synthesis for analysis framework, the cost functions of the initial fitting and the motion model fitting are

$$c_{motion}(\sigma, \lambda, c, R, t) = ||s^* - c(R(s + f\overrightarrow{\lambda}) + t)||_2, \tag{3.16}$$

where s^* is the 2D target landmark points.

This cost function is similar to the fitting cost function in Section 3.2 and is solved similarly. After processing on each frame, the visibility of the feature points is updated by checking z-buffer generated from the full model. Only the visible feature points in the previous frame are used for tracking the face in the next frame.

After the FAP values λ are recovered, they are used to reconstruct the full detail mesh by applying

3.3.4 *Experimental Results*

In our experiment, we train the initial fitting model on USF 3D dataset [Blanz and Vetter (1999)] which consists of 100 samples, normalized into 8955 vertices. For the test set, we use the publicly available BU-4DFE dataset [Yin *et al.* (2008)] to render videos of subjects with different expression and rigid movement. The BU-4DFE database was created at the State University of New York at Binghamton by Yin *et al.* This database captures the dynamics of 3D expressive facial surfaces over a time period of 101 subjects, including 58 females and 43 males of different ethnicity: Asian, Black, Hispanic/Latino, and White. For each subject, there are six 3D face model sequences corresponding to the six fundamental facial expressions (namely anger, disgust, happiness, fear, sadness, and surprise).

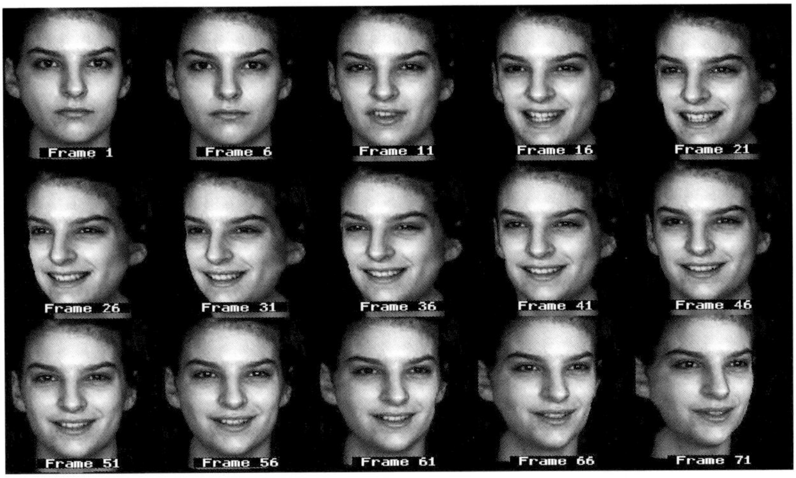

Fig. 3.12: Frames of generated video from BU-4DFE as test data.

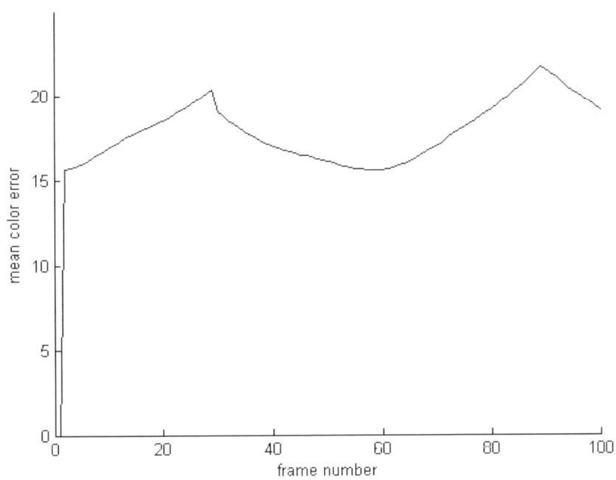

Fig. 3.13: Mean color error over the frames.

In each sequence, the face models are captured at the rate of 25 models per second. Each face model in a sequence contains the shape and texture of the subject during an expression period. All expression periods typically last about 4 seconds (approximately 100 frames).

With each sequence in the database, we set the first frame near frontal view, then gradually change the pan angle between -30 and 30 degrees, and translate in both directions over the frames. A sample of synthesized videos is demonstrated in Figure 3.12.

We have our algorithm running fully automatically on the test videos. For initial landmark detection, we employ the CompASM algorithm [Le *et al.* (2012)] to detect 83 landmark points. On the other frames, the landmarks are visually tracked by KLT optical flow algorithm [Lucas *et al.* (1981); Shi and Tomasi (1994)].

For quantitative evaluation, we compare the pixel values of the face areas in the input frames with those on rendered frames from the avatar. The root mean square error of the algorithm is $RMSE = 17.67$ where the pixel value ranges from 0 to 255. Equivalently, the mean signal-to-noise ratio is SNR = 23.18 dB.

In a more detailed analysis, we observe that the error does not distribute uniformly throughout the frames of the video. Figure 3.13 shows the mean RMSE over the input video frames. The errors are higher near the 30th and 90th frames. These are the frames with highest pan angles of 30 degrees. This phenomenon results from the fact that when the pose is farther from frontal, more landmark points are invisible. More importantly, at higher pose angles, the linearized assumptions are less valid, which introduces error to the approximated fitting algorithm.

Further indirect quantitative evaluation of the tracking algorithm will be reported in Chapter 6 by comparing the synthesized images with the original input video frames.

3.4 3D Face Modeling from RGB-D Images

3.4.1 *Introduction*

In the 3D model fitting and tracking algorithms introduced in Sections 3.2 and 3.3 in this chapter, the 3D information of the model is predicted from a 2D geometrical measure of landmark points with the help from the prior morphable model. Although requiring only universal available imaging devices, these 2D approaches have to predict 3D shape information purely from the statistical model. In several cases, this nature introduces instability and inaccuracy to the shape model fitting. They also require costly iterative procedures which concurrently optimize the body rigid transformation and facial deformation.

With the availability of the commodity 3D sensing devices such as Microsoft Kinect, Asus action pro, Intel perceptual computing camera, the active sensed depth signal can be acquired at low cost. The depth signal captured by these devices, although noisy, provides a reliable source of 3D information for the model. In this section, we introduce a new set of algorithms which take input as RGB-D images from the commodity 3D cameras and operate efficient and stable simultaneous alignment and deformation optimization for 3D dynamic model fitting.

3.4.2 *3D Face Model Fitting with RGB-D Signal*

In Section 3.2, we introduce our iterative linearized morphable fitting algorithm using 2D feature points detected from a single RGB frame. The algorithm enables predicting 3D geometric structure of the face from 2D cues by projecting the feature vectors from 2D landmark points to a linear subspace of 3D shape. Although efficient and robust to texture noise, the approach made an assumption that the variation in depth can be predicted from 2D geometry. Relying on this loose assumption sometimes leads the algorithm to unstable fitting results in difficult situations such as high pose angles. We propose to update this algorithm to work with RGB-D camera, in which the 3D feature points are extracted and guide the fitting process. The overall framework is depicted in Figure 3.14.

Although readily available from the devices, the depth measures given by commodity depth cameras are normally noisy and having holes. In order to get reliable 3D points for fitting algorithm, we have a preprocessing step of accumulating a sequence of depth frames and integrating them into one single model. This process is done in a simultaneous localization and mapping (SLAM) algorithm. We used the system presented by Meyer and Do in [Meyer and Do (2013)] for aggregate a set of noisy depth frames and build up a surface by volumetric representation.

After the raw models are reconstructed from a collection of frames, the 2D facial feature are extracted from one of the RGB frame used for building the model. They are then mapped to the point cloud for the 3D feature points. With the 3D feature points under the correspondence with the morphable model, we can fit the morphable model using an iterative procedure consisting of two steps. At the rigid body movement step, the 3D feature points are matched with the counterparts of the morphable model using SVD based 3D alignment technique [Arun *et al.* (1987)]. Comparing to the counterpart step in 2D fitting, this step can be done much more

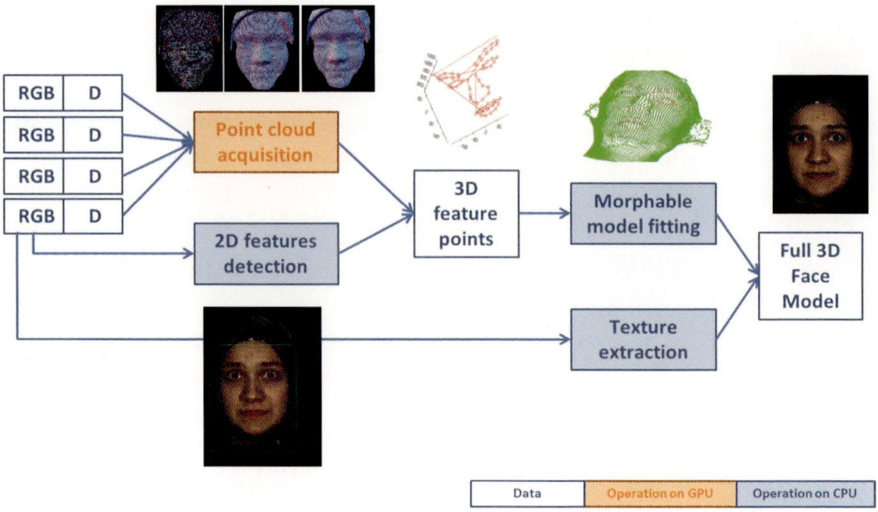

Fig. 3.14: Work flow of fitting 3D morphable face model from sequence of RGB-D image frames.

efficiently thank to the close form solution available for 3D point cloud alignment. At the second step of each iteration, we fit the 3D morphable model by projecting the residual of the aligned 3D feature map to the canonical space spanned by PCA model using Eq. 3.5 in Section 3.2.2.

3.4.3 *3D Face Model Tracking with RGB-D Signal*

When fitting the expressive model from 2D videos using the algorithm in Section 3.3, the depth components of the tracked feature points are generated from the statistical deduction. Therefore not only their accuracy is affected but also there is an apparent limitation on the FAPs related to only z direction, such as FAP 14 "Thrust_jaw" or FAP 16 "Push_bottom_lip". To alleviate the problem, we propose to update the tracking algorithms so that it can take advantage of the depth signal from RGBD cameras for more reliable tracking result.

In this method, the whole depth image region of the face is used by the ICP engine for rigid tracking. Although depth signals are noisy and not suitable for nonrigid detail tracking, the facial area of the depth frame provides enough information to the appearance based approach for reliable rigid motion estimation. We again use the implementation of Meyer and

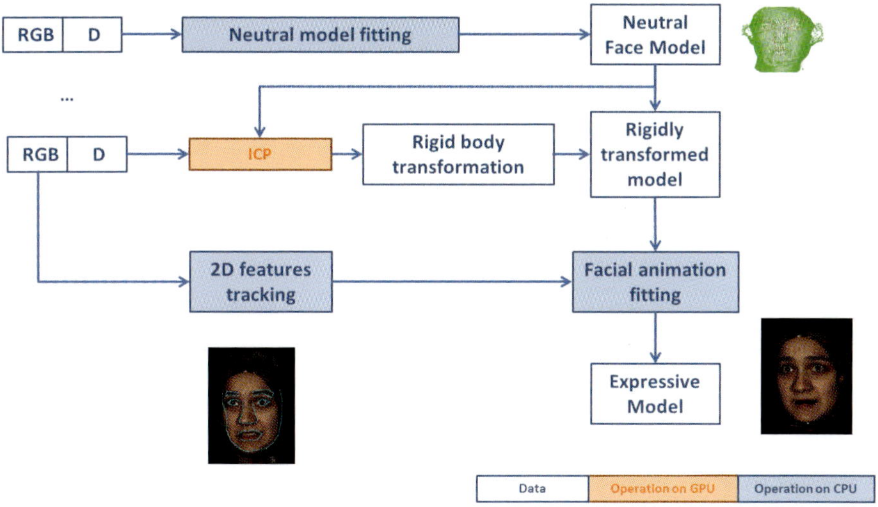

Fig. 3.15: Work flow of tracking and fit the expressive morphable face model from an RGB-D image frame.

Do [Meyer and Do (2013)] for efficient ICP alignment using GPUs. Concurrently, the 2D landmark points are visually tracked on RGB image using optical flow. The tracked landmarks are then used for the next step of nonrigid alignment by optimizing cost function 3.16 by linear least squares. Because the two processes are done on two different processing units: rigid tracking on GPU and nonrigid tracking on CPU, we have little overhead in computation. The procedure is further illustrated in Figure 3.15.

Although straightforward and efficient, the methods introduced may have to deal with the fact that the depth signal has a much higher noise level than the other two coordinates of landmark points. This challenge can be alleviated by filtering the depth signal with some smoothing kernel. The resolution of depth image is significantly larger than the number of feature points needed to track; therefore, the neighborhood area can have a good chance to give the feature point a better estimation of depth through filtering.

Also, in the proposed method, the two channels of the RGB-D images are processed separately and their processed results are combined by a late fusion style. Another interesting direction for early combining RGB and depth component is demonstrated in Figure 3.16. In this method, the salient feature points such as SIFT or SURF interest points are detected

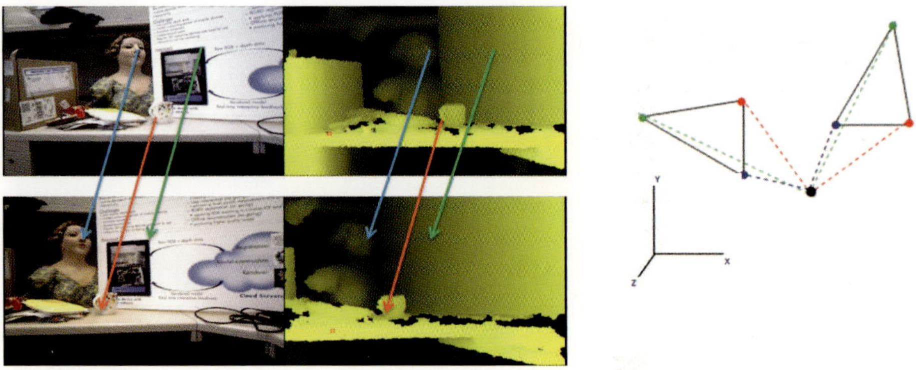

Fig. 3.16: Illustration of the collaboration of depth and RGB signal in reconstruction. The correspondences are found in RGB frame, mapped to depth frames and point clouds, then used for transformation estimation

on RGB images, they are then mapped to depth frame. The two 3D points set are then used to find alignment parameters. This direction will be investigated in future research.

3.5 Conclusions

In this chapter, we propose a novel algorithm for reconstructing the 3D shape and texture of human faces from an arbitrary single image or a pair of images captured from calibrated cameras. Subjective and quantitative evaluations have shown that the proposed algorithm is more efficient and accurate than the state of the art. With these promising results, our future work will generalize the current algorithm to the scenarios with more input images which will allow better geometry reconstruction and more complete texture, and integrate automatic feature point localization and camera self-calibration. We believe our work will be useful for building a fully automatic system of 3D face reconstruction, recognition and animation in practical applications.

We also introduced a new efficient, robust and accurate algorithm for nonrigid tracking of 3D shape model of human faces to a monocular video sequence. The algorithm is implemented into a complete fully automatic system running in real time on regular portable computers. The algorithm's outstanding efficiency and high performance show plentiful potential for animation and teleconference applications.

In the next chapters, we will investigate the use of geometry and motion recovered by the algorithm in eye gaze detection and avatar animation which are the keys in distance learning and other driving high quality photorealistic performance driven avatar and recognizing subject's emotion.

Chapter 4

Eye Gaze Estimation

4.1 Introduction

Along with facial expressions, eye gaze is another means by which humans can convey their cognitive and affective state. Eye gaze direction is particularly useful when trying to determine intent, making it a critical piece for analyzing levels of attentions and for navigating user interfaces, specifically for disabled patients. But while eye gaze is known to be extremely informative, it is also one of the most subtle cues for a computer to interpret and understand.

For instance, a person's head pose plays a key role in determining a person's perceived gaze direction. Studies conducted by [Langton *et al.* (2004)] and [Wollaston (1824)] showed that by affixing specific eye directions onto different head poses caused the observer's perception of the gaze direction to be heavily biased by the head pose. This process suggests that eye gaze direction is composed of two components: head pose and eyeball direction. Head pose provides a coarse estimation of the gaze direction while the eyeball provides a finer approximation. But despite its effect on gaze perception, head pose was not actively modeled in many of the early methods for gaze estimation. Most methods concentrated on specifically estimating the eyeball direction by fixing the head pose using chinrests or bite-bars. Only until fairly recently have gaze direction algorithms tried to actively incorporate head pose into their estimation procedures.

Another challenge for gaze estimation algorithms is adapting the framework to suit a diverse user population. While some model parameters are based on the scene geometry or are intrinsic camera properties, they only need to be measured once whereas human-specific properties such as inter-pupillary distance must be measured for each subject. This process of parameter estimation is known as calibration. The most desirable attributes for an eye tracker to achieve highly accurate estimates while allowing for free head movement and requiring minimal calibration [Hansen and Ji (2010)].

The traditional setting in which the eye gaze estimation algorithms are analyzed and evaluated involves having a subject sitting in front of one or more cameras, watching material being presented on a computer screen. The main goal of the algorithm is to determine the subject's point-of-gaze (PoG) on the screen using information inferred from the camera images. This mapping from visual data to PoG is clearly non-trivial and can be obtained in a variety of ways. The quality of the point estimate is then evaluated by computing the angular error between the estimated gaze direction and the true gaze direction.

4.2 Previous Work

Previous attempts to learn the mapping from image to gaze point can be broken up into four broad categories as indicated by [Hansen and Ji (2010)]. They include: (i) 2D feature-based techniques, (ii) 2D appearance-based models (iii) 3D geometric model-based techniques and (iv) visible light methods.

4.2.1 *Feature-based Methods*

As their name suggests, feature-based methods involve the use of hand-crafted or automatically detected features from input eye images and using them to train a classifier to learn the mapping from image to gaze point. Since the eye is a highly reflective object, specularities can cause a variety of problems for visible light methods. Therefore, the vast majority of feature-based methods use active lighting via infrared lights and sensors. Under infrared lighting, the contrast of the eye image improves considerably which greatly simplifies the task of segmenting the iris and pupil. The most common feature extracted from the infrared images is the reflected position of the illumination source, known as the glint.

In [Merchant *et al.* (1974)], [White *et al.* (1993)] and [Morimoto *et al.* (2000)], the authors proposed using the difference vector between the pupil and the glint as a feature and subsequently using polynomial regression to estimate the 2D coordinates of the gaze point. Later on, more sophisticated models such as neural networks [Zhu and Ji (2004)] and Support Vector Regressors (SVRs) [Zhu *et al.* (2006)] were used to perform the regression task. While successful to some degree, feature-based methods are not robust to head movement and therefore require more cameras [Zhu and Ji (2007)] to reliably learn the gaze mapping.

4.2.2 *Appearance-based Methods*

Unlike feature-based methods which use specific characteristics of the eye image as input to learn the gaze mapping, appearance-based models use the entire eye image. In [Baluja and Pomerleau (1994)], the authors use a neural network to directly learn the mapping while the authors in [Tan *et al.* (2002)] use a locally linear embedding (LLE). Both the methods, like the feature-based methods, used active (infrared) lighting to obtain their input eye images. Despite their relative simplicity, appearance methods require a large amount of calibration points and, like feature-based techniques, are not robust to head pose. Comparisons of feature-based and appearance-based methods are summarized in Figure 4.1.

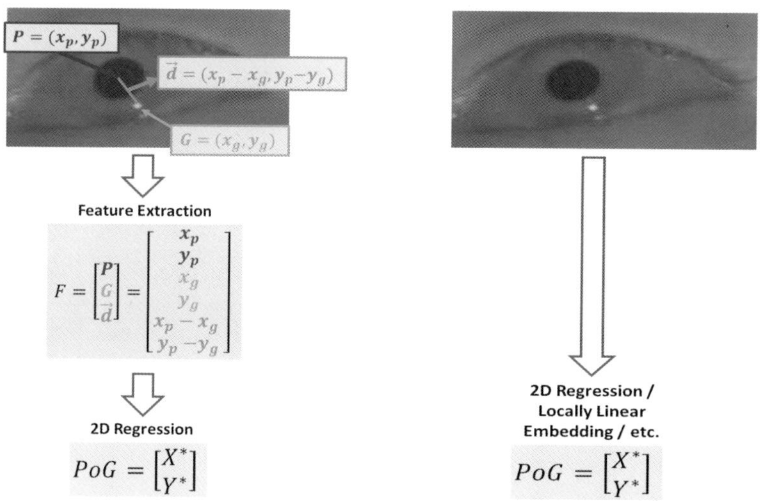

(a) Feature-based Methods (b) Appearance-based Methods

Fig. 4.1: Visual comparison of the gaze estimation algorithms — (a) Feature-based algorithms compute quantities such as the pupil center (P), glint position (G), and their displacement vector ($\vec{d}$), groups them into a feature vector and learns a mapping to the Point of Gaze (PoG) via regression. (b) Appearance-based methods try to directly relate the eye images to the PoG. Eye images taken from [Hansen and Ji (2010)].

4.2.3 *Geometric Model-based Methods*

Geometric model-based methods try to represent the 3D layout of the scene. Specifically, they compute a 3D gaze direction vector from measured characteristics of the subject's eye (cornea center, visual and optical axis) and try to intersect it with the object of interest (i.e. computer screen). One method by [Ohno *et al.* (2002)] proposed using a single IR camera coupled with a single IR light source to estimate the 3D gaze vector. The subject-specific parameters were approximated using population averages, but the method was not head-pose invariant. Work by [Shih *et al.* (2000)] and [Guestrin and Eizenman (2006)] showed that adding another light source significantly helped in achieving head-pose invariance. Multiple cameras solutions [Beymer and Flickner (2003)] [Brolly and Mulligan (2004)] have also been proposed to handle the problem of head pose by having one camera with a wide field of view capture head movement while a second camera with a narrow field of view capture the eyeball motion.

Another work developed by [Funes Mora and Odobez (2012)] used depth information extracted using a Kinect sensor to estimate the position of the subject's head in 3D space. This provided a coarse estimation of the subject's gaze direction which they subsequently refined by doing appearance-based estimation on the eyeball images. The method they selected was adaptive linear regression as suggested by [Lu *et al.* (2011)] but instead of weighting the eye images and their corresponding gaze points, the authors weighted the eye images and their gaze direction adjustment angles corresponding to eyeball yaw and tilt (ϕ, θ). The authors further improved this refinement process in [Funes Mora and Odobez (2013)]. Unfortunately, actively modeling the 3D layout of scene requires extensive calibration. Naturally this makes geometric model-based systems too cumbersome to deploy despite their impressive performance.

4.2.4 *Visible Light Methods*

Despite their many advantages in performance, the aforementioned techniques rely on the use of IR cameras and illuminators. Although the hardware components are widely available, the fashioning of the devices may prove to be too time-consuming for the average user. Natural light methods provide a far more accessible and intuitive alternative for gaze analysis. Almost all laptops and mobile devices come equipped with an RGB camera. Developing a reliable visible light based eye tracker could open the door to a wide array of applications across a large user base.

This area of research is still rather new, however there has been work in the last few years that has shown promising results. For instance, work by [Lu *et al.* (2011)] applied the ideas of appearance-based methods and combined them with sparse coding to estimate the final gaze point, while in [Nguyen *et al.* (2013)], the author's used a particle filter to track each of the eyes from frame to frame. Despite achieving low angular errors, these methods require that the user's head pose be fixed using a chin rest. The lack of head motion is, of course, rather unrealistic for most applications.

In 2012, a technique by Valenti *et al.* [Valenti *et al.* (2012)] actively incorporated head pose when estimating gaze, achieving excellent results. However their system does not operate in real-time. The main drawback of visible light techniques is that they are far less accurate than IR-based methods when estimating gaze direction ($\approx 5^\circ$ error vs. $\approx 1^\circ$ error), suggesting ample room for improvement. In the remainder of this chapter, we present a visible light technique that uses head pose to perform eye gaze estimation based on the system described in [Khorrami *et al.* (2014)]. We will show that our results are comparable to state-of-the-art methods [Valenti *et al.* (2012); Funes Mora and Odobez (2012)], which will support the claim made by [Langton *et al.* (2004)] that head pose is a coarse but accurate estimate of gaze direction.

4.3 Eye Gaze Estimation Using 3D Models

In this section, we propose to estimate the gaze point of the subject by reconstructing a geometric model of the 3D scene including the subject's face, the RGB camera and the screen. Using this scene model, we project a vector from the eyes, along the gaze direction. The intersection of the gaze vectors with the screen indicates the gaze point. In our setup, the positions of the screen and the camera are assumed to be fixed and predetermined. The remaining unknowns are the eye positions and gaze direction. Figure 4.2 illustrates how our proposed approach aims to estimate a person's gaze point. In our system, the gaze direction is determined by the subject's head pose. We estimate the head pose frame by frame using a 3D face tracking engine and subsequently compute the gaze point using perspective geometry. Our system operates in real-time and we verify the accuracy of the gaze point estimates in Section 4.4.

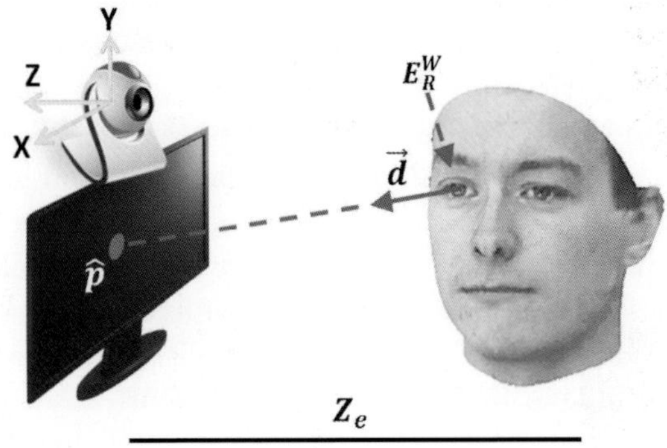

Fig. 4.2: Visualization of Gaze Direction Estimation Algorithm. The 3D world coordinates of the right eye (E_R^W) are computed from the image coordinates given by the face tracking algorithm. E_R^W is used as a starting point to construct the vector $\vec{d}$ whose direction is defined by the subject's head pose. The intersection point of $\vec{d}$ with the screen is the estimated gaze point $\hat{p}$.

4.3.1 *3D Face Model Tracking*

Following the modeling techniques introduced in Chapter 3, a personalized 3D morphable model of the subject is fit to the landmark points detected in the first frame of the video. These landmark points are then tracked in later frames and fed into the motion model. In our experiments, we use Lucas–Kanade optical flow [Shi and Tomasi (1994)] to visually track the 2D feature points. The motion recovered is then projected onto a deformation model based on MPEG4's Facial Animation Parameters [Ostermann (2002)]. This model regularizes the motion and infers the 3D morphing of the whole facial mesh. The high level workflow of the system is depicted in Figure 4.3.

With this tracking, we recover the global transformation parameters (translation and rotation) together with the 3D point mesh of the face. The location of two eyes in 3D space together with the pose direction of the face are extracted and will be used to infer the estimated gaze point. In particular, our method extracts the pixel locations of the two eyes as well as the head pose via pitch, yaw, and roll rotation angles (α, β, γ, respectively) of the head. Figure 4.4 illustrates the geometrical parameters recovered by our face tracking algorithm.

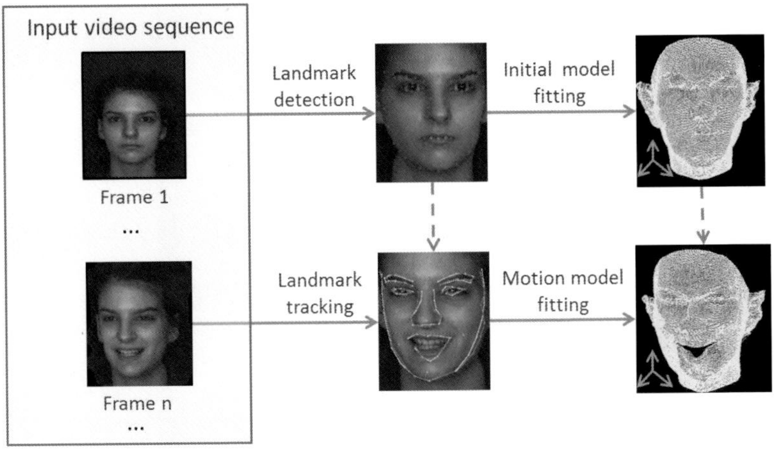

Fig. 4.3: Workflow of our face tracking algorithm. The first row shows the fitting process where a personalized morphable model is fit to a set of landmark points detected in the first frame of the video. The second row shows the tracking steps applied on later frames in which the tracked landmark points are used by a MPEG-4 facial motion model.

4.3.2 *Gaze Direction Estimation*

Using the 2D positions of the eyes given by our face tracker, our gaze estimation algorithm performs the following steps: (i) the 3D world coordinates of the subject's eyes are computed (ii) a direction vector ($\vec{d}$) from the eyes is constructed via the estimated head pose, (iii) we find the gaze point ($\hat{p}$) by computing the intersection point of the screen plane and the line originating from the subject's eyes and following the direction specified by $\vec{d}$. Figure 4.2 summarizes the steps of our algorithm and shows the aforementioned quantities as well as our conventions used for the image and world coordinate systems. We set the camera center to be the origin of the coordinate system and have the Z-axis be perpendicular to the image plane.

First, we calculate the 3D world coordinates of the subject's left and right eyes ($E_L^{\mathrm{W}}, E_R^{\mathrm{W}}$) using the pinhole camera model [Stockman and Shapiro (2001); Forsyth and Ponce (2002); Hartley and Zisserman (2003)]. This involves finding a correspondence between the location of the eyes in the world coordinate system and their pixel locations in the image ($E_L^{\mathrm{IMG}}, E_R^{\mathrm{IMG}}$). But, in order to properly estimate the 3D coordinates of a subject's eyes, we need to have extra information about the scene

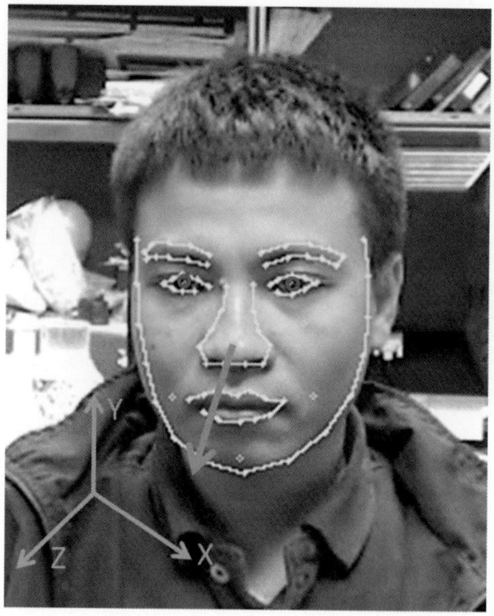

Fig. 4.4: 3D geometry recovered by our face tracking algorithm. The cyan dots show the tracked feature points; the red circles shows the 3D location of the two eyes; the blue arrow shows the estimated pose direction of the face. These features are relayed to the gaze point estimation module.

configuration to approximate the depth. Since the camera performs a perspective transform on the real world to construct an image, we know that lateral position in 3D (X) is related to lateral position in the image (u) via the following proportion given by similar triangles:

$$\frac{X_e}{Z_e} = \frac{u_e}{-f}, \tag{4.1}$$

$$Z_e = \frac{-f\, X_e}{u_e}, \tag{4.2}$$

where Z_e is the depth of the eye in millimeters, f is the focal length of the camera in pixels, u_e is the measured inter-pupillary distance in pixels, and X_e is the inter-pupillary distance in millimeters. X_e is estimated offline using population averages ($\approx$ 62.5 mm). Now if a subject's eyes have image coordinates $E_R^{\mathrm{IMG}} = (u_R, v_R)$ and $E_L^{\mathrm{IMG}} = (u_L, v_L)$, the coordinates of the eyes in the world coordinate system would be:

$$E_R^{\mathrm{W}} = \left(\frac{(u_R - u_0)Z_e}{-f}, \frac{(v_R - v_0)Z_e}{-f}, Z_e \right), \tag{4.3}$$

$$E_L^{\mathrm{W}} = \left(\frac{(u_L - u_0)Z_e}{-f}, \frac{(v_L - v_0)Z_e}{-f}, Z_e \right). \tag{4.4}$$

With the positions of the eyes in hand, we now determine the gaze direction vector ($\vec{d}$) by constructing a rotation matrix R_F using the extracted head pose angles (α, β, γ) and multiplying it by the Z-axis. Since each head pose angle defines an elementary rotation about one of the world coordinate axes, each rotation angle has its own corresponding rotation matrix $(R_X(\alpha), R_Y(\beta), R_Z(\gamma))$. These matrices are then multiplied together to form the full rotation matrix R_F in the following manner:

$$R_F = R_Y(\beta) \cdot R_X(\alpha) \cdot R_Z(\gamma). \tag{4.5}$$

Multiplying R_F by the Z-axis gives the pose direction vector:

$$\vec{d} = R_F \begin{bmatrix} 0 \\ 0 \\ 1 \end{bmatrix} = \begin{bmatrix} \cos(\alpha)\sin(\beta) \\ -\sin(\alpha) \\ \cos(\alpha)\cos(\beta) \end{bmatrix}. \tag{4.6}$$

The estimated gaze point is subsequently defined as the point of intersection between the screen (Z=0) and the line constructed with the direction vector $\vec{d}$ originating from the left eye or the right eye point, E_L^{W} or E_R^{W}. The two estimated intersection points $\hat{P}_R$ and $\hat{P}_L$ are calculated in Eq. 4.7 and 4.8 and the final gaze point estimate ($\hat{P}_{\mathrm{AVG}}$) is simply the average of the two (Eq. 4.9).

$$\hat{P}_R = E_R^{\mathrm{W}} + \left(\frac{-Z_e}{\cos(\alpha)\cos(\beta)} \right) \vec{d}, \tag{4.7}$$

$$\hat{P}_L = E_L^{\mathrm{W}} + \left(\frac{-Z_e}{\cos(\alpha)\cos(\beta)} \right) \vec{d}, \tag{4.8}$$

$$\hat{P}_{\mathrm{AVG}} = \frac{\hat{P}_R + \hat{P}_L}{2}. \tag{4.9}$$

4.4 Experiments

We will now discuss the experiments we conducted to verify the accuracy of our gaze estimation system. Unfortunately, there exist very few publicly available gaze estimation datasets that are suited for the Point of Gaze (PoG) estimation problem. Oftentimes the datasets do not contain enough subjects or do not adequately span the space of possible gaze directions. Work by [Weidenbacher *et al.* (2007)] and [Smith *et al.* (2013)], however tried to directly address these deficiencies by using many subjects (20 and 56 respectively) and several orientations for head pose and eyeball direction. The main limitation of these two datasets was that they only gave still images of each direction rather videos, making them unsuitable for evaluating tracking-based solutions. On the other hand, in [Asteriadis *et al.* (2009)] and [McMurrough *et al.* (2012)], the authors present datasets that create video sequences of their subjects by accurately tracking their head pose using head-mounted hardware (LEDs and reflective markers respectively). While more suitable for tracking-based algorithms, these datasets do not consider enough gaze positions (3 and 9 respectively) to gain an in-depth analysis on performance.

Therefore, to address the aforementioned issues, we constructed our own dataset and acquisition protocol. We collected data from 10 subjects sitting approximately 800 mm away using a webcam in a natural manner. For each acquisition trial, we broke the screen area into a 6×7 grid and instructed the user to follow a sequence of highlighted rectangular regions over a pre-specified or random path by moving their head. The trials consisted of two pre-specified paths and two random paths to simulate different types of head movement sequences. Figure 4.5 provides an example pre-specified path used during the evaluations.

As each subject followed the colored block across the screen, the webcam captured their head movements and stored the images as a video. The face tracking module then used this video to compute the subject's eye locations and head pose angles for each frame and stored them along with the pixel location of the displayed block's center as ground truth. We used a Logitech c920 webcam and a computer monitor with resolution 1680×1050 pixels to capture the data. One advantage of our system is that it does not require calibration before every trial. Only the camera focal length is needed and only needed to be measured once.

We measured the accuracy of our gaze algorithm by computing the mean absolute error (MAE) between the estimated gaze point and the ground truth point for each subject and average the results over all 4 trials. The average error values for each subject are displayed in Table 4.1. Our final mean error in the x and y directions over all the subjects is (273.78, 308.9) pixels which corresponds to angles of ($5.91°$, $6.40°$) respectively. Our method achieve a lower average angular error ($6.16°$) than the error reported in [Funes Mora and Odobez (2012)] ($14.83°$) and is comparable

Fig. 4.5: Sample path used for collecting gaze data. Each block is shown for two seconds and a webcam captures the subject's head movements as they follow the blocks across the screen.

to results presented in [Valenti *et al.* (2012)]. While the method proposed in [Valenti *et al.* (2012)] achieves lower average angular errors (4.6°, 4.7°) which correspond to MAEs of (210.33, 214.99) in the x and y directions, their technique is not real-time and requires some offline processing.

Table 4.1: Average gaze estimation errors for all 10 subjects. The first two columns give the Mean Absolute Error (MAE) of the estimated gaze points in x and y directions. The third column gives Average Mean Absolute Error (All values are in units of pixels.)

Subject	MAE_X	MAE_Y	MAE_{AVG}
1	266.61	274.32	270.46
2	275.16	429.46	352.31
3	249.54	502.77	376.16
4	173.58	209.44	191.51
5	307.37	290.93	299.15
6	317.02	323.00	320.01
7	307.49	372.62	340.06
8	265.66	195.53	230.60
9	368.97	247.90	308.44
10	206.38	242.99	224.69
Average	273.78	308.90	291.34

4.5 Conclusions

In this chapter, we discussed previous advancements in the area of eye gaze estimation. We analyzed the rise of visible light methods as a possible new area of research and presented our own technique that uses head pose as a rough estimate for approximating gaze direction. We further showed how our method obtains results that are comparable or superior to the current state-of-the-art. In Chapter 7, we will discuss how this technique can be used to analyze the attentive state of remote students in a classroom setting.

Chapter 5

Expressive Audio-visual Avatar

5.1 Introduction

Expressive audio-visual avatars are humanoid computer-based virtual agents which act and speak just like human beings. Such humanoid avatars introduce the presence of individuals to capture attention, mediate conversational cues, and communicate emotional affect, personality and identity in many application scenarios in the real world. They provide realistic-looking facial expressions and natural-sounding expressive speech to help people to enhance their understanding of the content and intent of the messages that they deliver. Undoubtedly, if modern computers are embodied and represented by expressive audio-visual avatars, the quality of human–computer interaction (HCI) can be significantly improved. In addition, personalized expressive audio-visual avatars may also serve as personal assistants for individuals with speech and hearing problems to enable them to participate in daily communications [Huang *et al.* (2009); Fu *et al.* (2010)].

The use of avatars has emerged in the market place in the last decade. However, the understanding of human communications has not yet advanced to the point where it is possible to make realistic avatars that demonstrate interactions with natural-sounding expressive speech and realistic-looking facial expressions. The key research issues which enable avatars to communicate subtle or complex emotions include how to synthesize natural-sounding expressive speech, how to animate realistic-looking facial expressions, and how to combine lip motion with facial expressions in a natural and realistic fashion [Tang *et al.* (2008a)].

In this chapter, we describe our past research that had led to the development of a system framework and methods for constructing a 3D text-driven expressive audio-visual avatar [Tang *et al.* (2008b)]. This is an interdisciplinary research area that is related to speech, computer graphics and computer vision. This chapter is organized as follows: In Section 5.2, we review previous work that is related to various aspects of our research. In Section 5.3, we describe the system framework and methods that lead to a 3D text-driven expressive audio-visual avatar. In Section 5.4, we demonstrate the effectiveness of our system and evaluate its performance with subjective experiments. We finally conclude this chapter and discuss how potential future improvements can be made to the system in Section 5.5.

5.2 Related Work

In this section, we perform a detailed review of the previous work related to the three key research issues, namely, how to synthesize natural-sounding expressive speech, how to animate realistic-looking facial expressions, and how to combine lip motion with facial expressions in a natural and realistic fashion.

5.2.1 *Expressive Speech Synthesis*

Attempts to add emotions to synthetic speech have existed for over a decade. Cahn [Cahn (1989)] and Murray [Murray (1989)] both used a commercial formant synthesizer (i.e., DECTalk) to generate expressive speech based on the emotion-specific acoustic parameter settings that they derived from the literature. Burkhardt [Burkhardt (2000)] also employed a formant synthesizer to synthesize expressive speech. Instead of deriving the acoustic profiles from the literature, he conducted perception-oriented experiments to find optimal values for the various parameters. Although partial success was achieved, reduced naturalness was reported due to the imperfect rules inherent with formant synthesis.

Several later undertakings and smaller studies have made use of the diphone synthesis approach. Schröder [Schröder (2004)] used a diphone synthesizer to model a continuum of intensity-varying emotional states under the emotion dimension framework. He searched for acoustic correlates of emotions by analysis of a carefully labeled emotional speech database and established a mapping of the points in the emotion space to their acoustic correlates. These acoustic correlates are then used to tune the prosodic parameters in the diphone synthesizer to generate expressive speech. The synthesized speech is observed to convey only non-extreme emotions and thus cannot be considered successful if it is used alone. Complimentary channels such as facial expressions are required to be used together in order for the user to fully comprehend the emotional state.

One might want to model a few "well-defined" emotion categories as close as possible, and it seems unit selection synthesis based on emotion-specific speech database can be a suitable choice for this purpose. Iida [Iida (2002)] built a separate speech database for each of three emotional states (angry, happy and sad) for a Japanese unit selection speech synthesizer (i.e., CHART). During synthesis, only units from the database corresponding to the specified emotional state are selected. Iida reported fairly good results of this method (60% to 80% emotion recognition rate). Hofer [Hofer (2004)] pursued a similar approach. He recorded separate speech databases for neutral as well as happy and angry styles. Pitrelli *et al.* at IBM [Pitrelli *et al.* (2006)] recorded a large database of neutral speech containing 11 hours of data as well as several relatively smaller databases of expressive speech (1 hour of data for each database). Instead of selecting units from one particular database at run time, they blended all the databases together and selected units from the blended database according to some criterion. They assumed that many of the segments comprising a sentence, spoken expressively, could come from the neutral database. This approach has demonstrated promising results.

Expressive speech synthesis is a very difficult research area. People have tried to compare speech synthesis with computer graphics: which is harder? Although the answer depends, at least in part, on one's definition of the word "harder," it is uncontroversial to state that current technology fools the eye more easily than it fools the ear. For example, computer graphics are widely accepted by the movie industry, while TTS synthesis still has a very long way to go until the synthetic speech can completely replace the real speech of an actor or actress [Schröder (2004)].

5.2.2 *3D Face Modeling and Animation*

The modeling of 3D facial geometry and deformation has been an active research topic for computer graphics and computer vision [Parke (1972); Wen and Huang (2004); Blanz and Vetter (1999); Hong *et al.* (2002)]. In the past, people have used interactive tools to design geometric 3D face models under the guidance of prior knowledge. As laser-based 3D range scanning products, such as the Cyberware^{TM} scanner, have become commercially available, people have been able to measure the 3D geometry of the human faces. The Cyberware^{TM} scanner shines a low-intensity laser beam onto the face of a subject and rotates around his or her head for 360 degrees. The 3D shape of the face can be recovered from the lighted profiles of every angle. With the measurement of 3D face geometry available, geometric 3D face models can be constructed [Wen and Huang (2004)]. Alternatively, a number of researchers have proposed to build 3D face models from 2D images using computer vision based techniques [Hong *et al.* (2001); Wen and Huang (2004); Fu and Zheng (2006); Tang *et al.* (2008c)]. Usually, in order to reconstruct 3D face geometry, multiple 2D images from different views are required. 3D range scanners, though very expensive, are able to provide high-quality measurement of 3D face geometry and thus enable us to construct realistic 3D face models. Reconstruction from 2D images, despite its noisy results, provides an alternative lost-cost approach to build 3D face models.

A geometric 3D face model determines the 3D geometry of a static facial shape. By spatially and temporally deforming the geometric face model we can obtain dynamic facial expressions changing over time. The facial deformation is controlled by a facial deformation model. The free-form interpolation model is one of the most popular facial deformation models in the literature [Hong *et al.* (2001); Tao and Huang (1999)]. In the free-form interpolation model, a set of control points are defined on the 3D geometry of the face model and any facial deformation is achieved through proper displacements of these control points. The displacements of the rest of the facial geometry can be obtained by a certain interpolation scheme. To impose constraints to the facial deformation space, linear subspace methods have been proposed. One example is the facial action coding system (FACS) [Ekman and Friesen (1977); Ekman *et al.* (1993)] which approximates arbitrary facial deformation as a linear combination of action units (AUs) [Pandzic and Forchheimer (2002)]. The AUs are qualitatively defined based on anatomical studies of the facial muscular activities that cause facial movements. Often, extensive and tedious manual work has to be done to create the AUs. As more and more facial motion capture data become available, it is possible to learn the subspace bases from the real-world data which are able to capture the characteristics of real facial deformations. Hong *et al.* [Hong *et al.* (2002)] applied principal component analysis (PCA) to real facial motion capture data and derived a few bases called motion units (MUs). Any arbitrary facial deformation can then be approximated by a linear combination of the MUs. Compared with the

AUs, the MUs are automatically derived from real-world data. Therefore, labor-intensive manual work can be avoided. In addition, the MUs have been proven to yield smaller reconstruction error than the AUs.

5.2.3 *Co-articulation of Lip Motion and Facial Expressions*

In an expressive audio-visual avatar, it is unclear how lip motion (due to speech production) are dynamically combined with facial expressions to ensure natural, realistic and coherent appearance. There is no theoretical grounding for determining the interactions and relative contributions of these respective sources that together cause facial deformation. Some researchers [Cao *et al.* (2005); Kshirsagar *et al.* (2001)] have used techniques like independent component analysis (ICA) and PCA to separate and model the viseme and expression spaces. However, neither is based on the theoretical grounding for determining the interactions and relative contributions of the respective sources that together cause facial deformation.

5.3 System Framework and Methods

In this section, we describe in detail the system framework and methods that lead to a 3D text-driven expressive audio-visual avatar.

5.3.1 *System Framework*

Our research has led to a system framework, as illustrated in Figure 5.1, toward building a 3D text-driven expressive audio-visual avatar. In the framework, an input textual message is first converted into expressive synthetic speech by an expressive speech synthesis module. At the same time, a phoneme sequence with exact timing is generated. The phoneme sequence is then mapped into a viseme sequence that defines the lip motion sequence. The emotional state associated with the input message decides the facial expressions, which will be combined with the lip motion sequence synchronously and naturally. A key frame interpolation technique is then used to animate the viseme sequence. Within the framework, our research focuses include facial expression animation, lip motion synthesis, co-articulation of lip motion and facial expressions, and expressive speech synthesis.

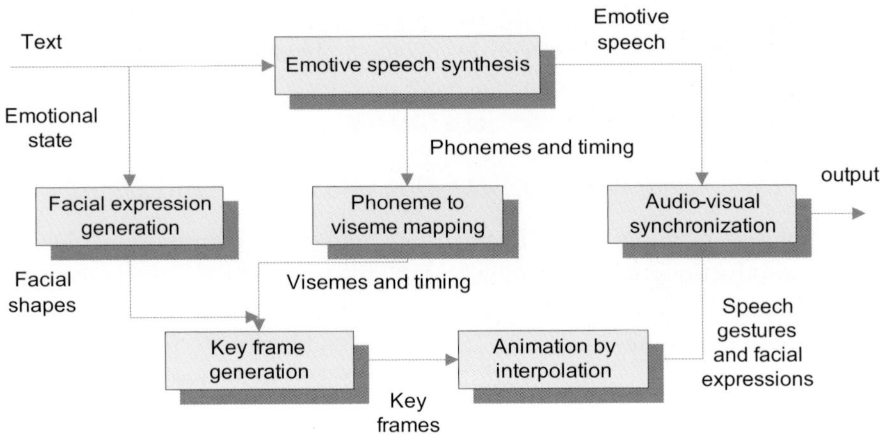

Fig. 5.1: System framework for 3D text-driven expressive audio-visual avatar.

5.3.2 *3D Face Modeling*

3D face modeling concerns the problem of how to represent the 3D geometry and texture of a human face, which is the essential foundation for any 3D face animation task. The UIUC iFace system provides a research platform for 3D face modeling [Hong *et al.* (2001, 2002)]. It takes as input the Cyberware^{TM} scanner data of a person's face and fits the data with a generic head model. The output is a customized geometric 3D face model ready for 3D face animation.

The generic head model, as shown in Figure 5.2, consists of the components of the head (i.e., face, eyes, ears, teeth, tongue, etc.). The surfaces of these components are approximated by triangular meshes. There are a total of 2240 vertices and 2946 triangles to ensure the closeness of the approximation. In order to customize the generic head model for a particular person, we need to obtain the range map (Figure 5.3, left) and texture map (Figure 5.3, right) of that person by scanning his or her face using a Cyberware^{TM} scanner. On the face component of the generic head model, 35 feature points are explicitly defined. If we were to unfold the face component onto a 2D plane, those feature points would triangulate the whole face into multiple local patches. By manually selecting 35 corresponding feature points on the texture map (and thus on the range map), as shown in Figure 5.3, right, we can compute the 2D positions of all the vertices of the

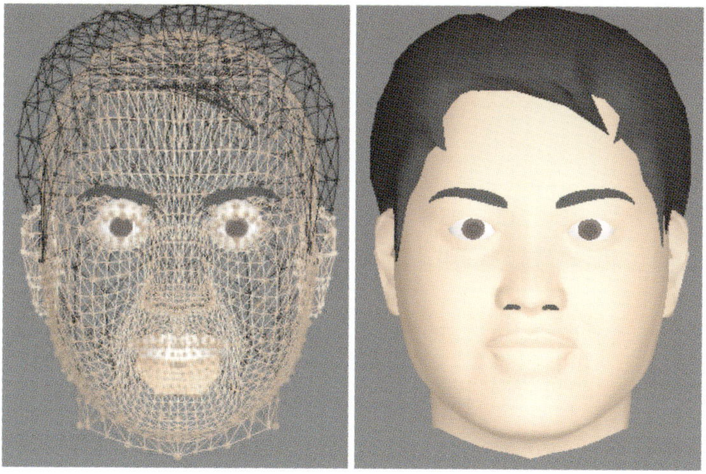

Fig. 5.2: Generic head model. (Left): Shown as wired. (Right): Shown as shaded.

face meshes in the range and texture maps. As the range map contains the 3D face geometry of the person, we can then deform the face component of the generic head model by displacing the vertices of the triangular meshes by certain amounts as determined by the corresponding range information collected at the corresponding positions. The remaining components of the generic head model (hair, eyebrows, etc.) are automatically adjusted by shifting, rotating and scaling. Manual adjustments and fine tunes are needed where the scanner data are missing or noisy. Figure 5.4, left, shows a personalized head model. In addition, texture can be mapped onto the customized head model to achieve photo-realistic appearance, as shown in Figure 5.4, right.

5.3.3 *3D Face Animation*

The 3D face model described in the previous subsection can be animated using techniques described in this subsection, as follows.

5.3.3.1 *Facial Expression Synthesis/Animation*

On the 3D face model, we define a control model, as shown in Figure 5.5. The control model is then used to synthesis/animate the 3D face

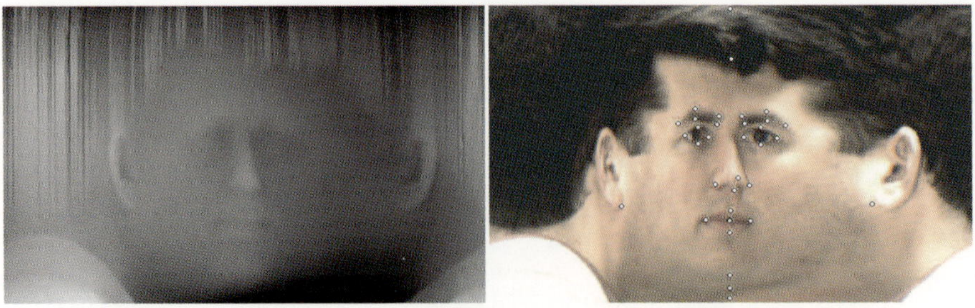

Fig. 5.3: Example of Cyberware^{TM} scanner data. (Left): Range map. (Right): Texture map with 35 feature points defined on it.

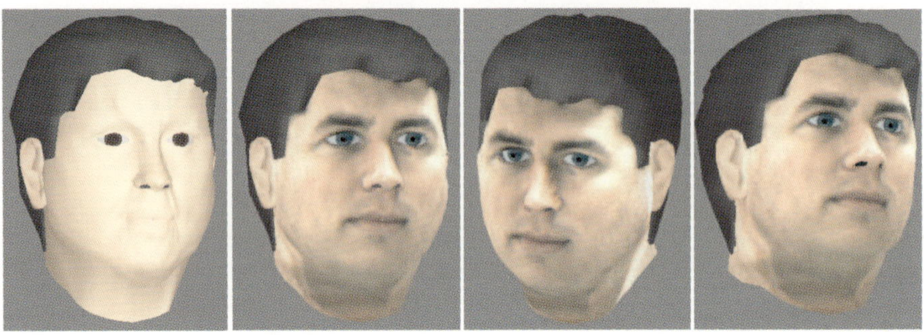

Fig. 5.4: Customized face model. (Left): No texture. (Right): Texture is mapped onto the model with several different poses.

model. The control model consists of 101 vertices and 164 triangles which cover the whole face region. It divides the face region into various local patches. By moving the vertices of the control model, one can deform the 3D face model into arbitrary shapes. As shown in Figure 5.6, a set of basic facial shapes corresponding to six different fullblown facial expressions are obtained in this way and parameterized as the displacements of all the vertices of the face model from their initial values corresponding to the neutral state. Let those displacements be $\Delta\vec{V}_i, i = 1, 2, \ldots, N$, where N is the number of vertices of the face model. The vertices of the deformed face model are given by $\vec{V}_{0i} + \rho \times \Delta\vec{V}_i, i = 1, 2, \ldots, N$, where $\vec{V}_{0i}$ are the vertices of the neutral face and $0 \leq \rho \leq 1$ is the magnitude coefficient representing the intensity of the facial expression. Here, $\rho = 1.0$ corresponds to the fullblown emotional facial expression while $\rho = 0.0$ corresponds to the neutral expression.

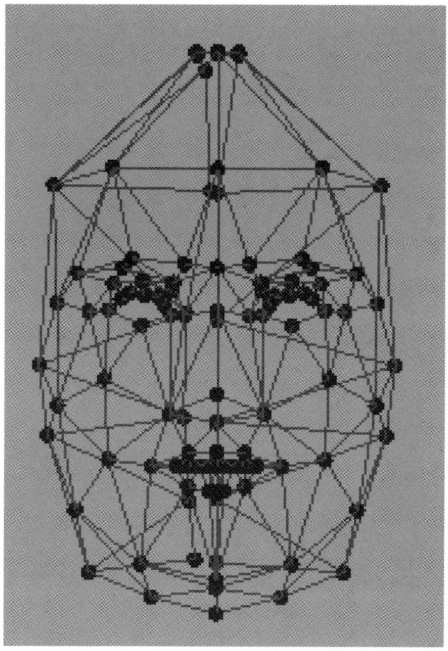

Fig. 5.5: Control model defined by 101 vertices and 164 triangles on the 3D face model.

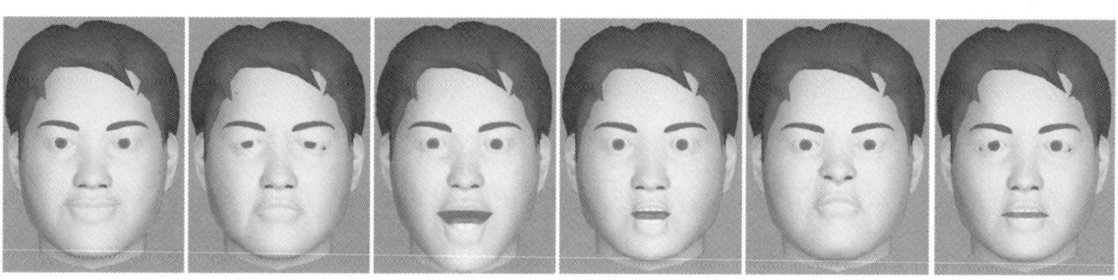

Fig. 5.6: A set of basic facial shapes corresponding to different fullblown emotional facial expressions.

5.3.3.2 *Lip Motion Synthesis/Animation*

We implement lip motion via visemes. We define a total of 17 visemes, each of which corresponds to one or more of the 40 phonemes in American English. Note that the phoneme-to-viseme mapping is not one-to-one. Different phonemes can be mapped to the same viseme provided that they are articulated in a similar manner. Table 5.1 lists all the phonemes and the corresponding visemes that they are mapped to. Phoneme-to-viseme mapping can thus be done by simple table look-up.

Table 5.1: Phonemes, examples, and corresponding visemes. Phoneme-to-viseme mapping can thus be done by simple table look-up.

Phoneme	Example	Viseme	Phoneme	Example	Viseme
i	beet	IY	I	bit	AX
E	bet	AY	{	bat	AE
r=	above	AX	u	boot	W
U	book	AX	V	above	AX
O	caught	AO	A	father	AA
@	butter	AX	EI	bay	NE
AI	bye	AY	OI	boy	T
aU	about	AY	@U	boat	OW
p	pan	M	t	tan	T
k	can	T	b	ban	M
d	dan	T	g	gander	T
m	me	M	n	knee	T
N	sing	AY	f	fine	F
T	thigh	TH	s	sign	T
S	assure	SH	h	hope	AY
v	vine	F	D	thy	TH
z	resign	T	Z	azure	SH
tS	church	SH	dZ	judge	SH
l	lent	LL	r	rent	R
j	yes	T	w	went	W
_	(silent)	NE			

5.3.3.3 *Co-articulation of Lip Motion and Facial Expressions*

The human facial muscular activities are very complex. How the movements of the lower face are together controlled by both speech production and facial expressions is still an open research problem. In situations where there is only the neutral facial expression, the movements of the lower face is assumed to be dominated by speech production. However, problems occur when emotional facial expressions are taken into account as in an expressive audio-visual avatar. Due to the highly dynamic nature of lip motion and facial expressions, the exact interactions and contributions of these two sources that control facial movements are unknown. We propose a linear combination approach by assuming that lip motion and facial expressions contribute equally (or weighted equally) to facial deformations. This assumption however can lead to faulty results (e.g., the mouth will never close while laughing and speaking). Another approach we propose is to treat the upper face and low face separately and assume that the upper face is mostly controlled by facial expressions while the lower face is mainly due to lip motion. This assumption is however subject to suspicion. Yet another approach we propose is to use nonlinear combination instead of linear combination, but rarely is known about how to find the underlying nonlinear function. An ad hoc solution is adopted: We first use the linear combination approach and then identify the top co-articulation difficulties between lip motion and facial expressions. We then "fix" these difficulties by manually creating "expressive visemes." This approach, though not very systematic, can often work well in practice.

5.3.4 *Expressive Speech Synthesis*

We adopt a diphone-based speech synthesizer and a differential approach for prosody modification to synthesize expressive speech [Tang *et al.* (2008d)]. The ability of diphone-based speech synthesis to control the prosodic parameters for speech synthesis is a very attractive property that can enable the generation of emotional affect in synthetic speech by explicitly modeling the particular emotion. In order to produce high-quality synthetic speech, a speech synthesis system usually consists of two main components: a natural language processing (NLP) module and digital signal processing (DSP) module. The NLP module performs necessary text analysis and prosody prediction procedures to convert orthographical text into proper phonetic transcription (i.e., phonemes) together with the desired intonation and rhythm (i.e., prosody). There are numerous methods that have been proposed and implemented for the NLP module. The DSP module takes as input the phonetic transcription and prosodic description which are the output of the NLP module, and transforms them into a speech signal. Likewise, various DSP techniques have been proposed for this purpose [Dutoit (1997)].

5.3.4.1 *Framework*

The general framework for expressive speech synthesis using a diphone-based speech synthesizer and a differential approach is illustrated in Figure 5.7. In this framework, an emotion transformer is inserted into the functional diagram of a general speech synthesis system and acts as a bridge that connects the NLP and DSP modules. The NLP module generates phonemes and prosody corresponding to the neutral state (i.e., neutral prosody). The emotion transformer aims to transform the neutral prosody into the desired emotional prosody as well as to transform the voice quality of the synthetic speech. The phonemes and emotional prosody are then passed on to the DSP module to synthesize expressive speech using a diphone-based speech synthesizer. Many aspects of this framework, especially the techniques, methods, and algorithms engaged in the NLP and DSP modules, have been thoroughly discussed in the literature [Dutoit (1997)]. In the following, we focus on several aspects of this framework that have not yet been extensively investigated.

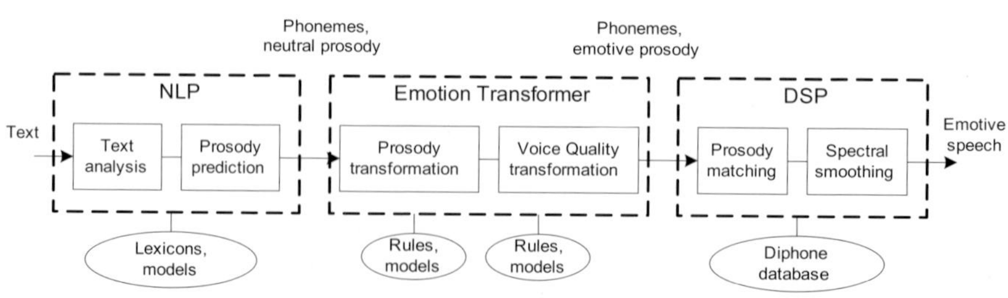

Fig. 5.7: General framework of emotive TTS synthesis using a diphone-based speech synthesizer.

5.3.4.2 *Prosody Transformation*

We introduce a differential approach for prosody transformation [Tang *et al.* (2008d)]. This approach aims to find the differences in prosody of the various emotional states with respect to the neutral state. The emotion transformer either maintains a set of prosody manipulation rules that define the variations of prosodic parameters between the neutral prosody and the expressive one, or trains a set of statistical prosody prediction models that predict these parameter variations given the features representing a particular textual context. The basic idea is formulated as $\Delta p = p_{\mathrm{e}} - p_{\mathrm{n}}$, where Δp denotes parameter difference, p_{n} denotes neutral prosodic parameter, and p_{e} denotes emotional prosodic parameter. During synthesis, the rules or the prediction outputs of the models will be applied to the neutral prosody, obtained via the NLP module. The emotional prosody can thus be obtained by adding to the neutral prosody the predicted variations. The basic idea is formulated as $\widehat{p_{\mathrm{e}}} = \widehat{p_{\mathrm{n}}} + \widehat{\Delta p}$, where $\widehat{\Delta p}$ denotes the predicted parameter difference, $\widehat{p_{\mathrm{n}}}$ denotes the predicted neutral prosodic parameter, and $\widehat{p_{\mathrm{e}}}$ denotes the predicted emotional prosodic parameter.

Compared with a "full" approach that aims to find the emotional prosody directly, the differential approach has several advantages. First, the differences of the prosodic parameters between the neutral prosody and the emotional ones have far smaller dynamic ranges than the prosodic parameters themselves and therefore the differential approach requires far less data to train the models than the full approach (e.g., 15 minutes versus several hours). Second, the differential approach makes possible the derivation of the prosody manipulation rules which are hardly possible to be obtained in the full approach.

In our differential approach, prosody transformation is achieved through applying a set of prosody manipulation rules. The prosody of speech can be manipulated at various levels. High-level prosody modification refers to the change of symbolic prosodic description of a sentence (i.e., human readable intonation and rhythm) which by itself does not contribute much to expressive speech synthesis unless there is a cooperative prosody synthesis model (i.e., a model that maps high-level symbolic prosodic description to low-level prosodic parameters). Low-level prosody modification refers to the direct manipulation of prosodic parameters, such as f_0, duration, and energy, which can lead to immediate perception of emotional affect. Macro-prosody (suprasegmental prosody) modification refers to the adjustment of global prosody settings such as mean, range and variability as well as the speaking rate, while micro-prosody (segmental prosody) modification refers to the modification to local segmental prosodic parameters which are probably related to the underlying linguistic structure of a sentence. It should be noted that not all levels of prosody manipulations can be described by rules. For instance, due to the highly dynamic nature of prosody variation, micro-prosody modification cannot be summarized by a set of rules. In our system, we choose to perform low-level micro-prosody modification. The global prosody settings that we use are given in Table 5.2, and pictorially shown in an example in Figure 5.8. These settings are adopted from those used in [Burkhardt (2005)], and Table 5.3 shows the prosody manipulation rules that we use in the system.

The values of global prosody modification parameters were first derived from previous work [Schröder (2004); Cahn (1989); Murray (1989); Burkhardt (2005)] and then carefully adjusted according to extensive listening experiments. Since these parameters are closely related to human

Table 5.2: Global prosody settings.

Parameter	Description
f_0 mean	mean value of f_0 contour, in Hz
f_0 range	difference between max. and min. values of f_0 contour
f_0 variability	degree of variation of f_0 contour
f_0 contour shape	shape of f_0 contour (rising, falling or level)
speaking rate	duration of speech

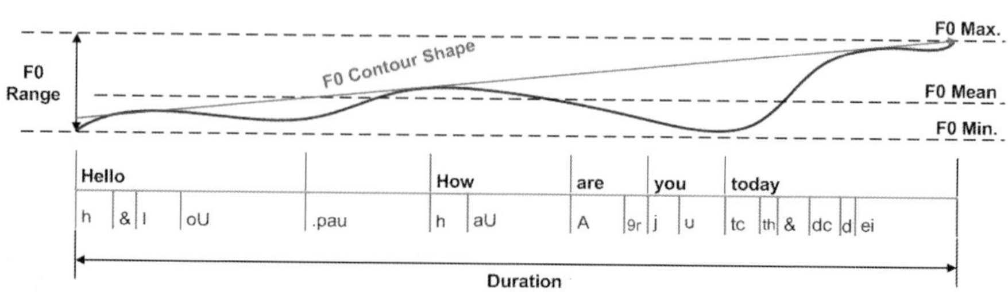

Fig. 5.8: Pictorial demonstration of global prosody settings. The blue curve is the f_0 contour, and the red straight line represents the f_0 contour shape.

Table 5.3: Prosody modification rules.

Manipulation of	Description
f_0 mean	shift the f_0 mean by multiplying all f_0 values by a factor
f_0 range	widen or narrow the f_0 range by shifting each f_0 value by a percentile of its distance to the f_0 mean
f_0 variability	increase or decrease the global f_0 variability by adjusting the f_0 range of each syllable
f_0 contour shape	reshape the f_0 contour on either phrase or syllable level by making it rise or fall controlled by a gradient
speaking rate	lengthen or shorten the duration of speech at various levels: global phrase level; syllable level based on stress type (unstressed, word-stressed, phrase-stressed); sound level based on category (vowels, diphthongs, nasals, fricatives, stops, etc.)

perception and user experience, we have used individual perceptual experiments to decide their perceptually best values. The performance of the system relies on these empirical values. However, due to the tolerance capability of human perception, there is a tolerance interval for each of these parameters. Our listening experiments confirm that small deviations of these parameters from their perceptually best values would not cause noticeable performance degradation.

5.3.4.3 *Voice Quality Transformation*

Several studies in the literature indicate that in addition to prosody transformation, voice quality transformation is important for synthesizing expressive speech and may be indispensable for certain emotion categories [Montero *et al.* (1999)]. In the diphone-based speech synthesis method, however, it is not easy to control voice quality, as it is very difficult to modify the voice quality of a diphone database. However, one partial remedy to alleviate this difficulty is to record separate diphone databases with different vocal efforts [Schröder and Grice (2003)]. At synthesis time, the system switches among different voice-quality diphone databases and selects the diphone units from the appropriate database. Another low-cost partial remedy is to use jitters to simulate voice quality transformation. Jitters are fast fluctuations of the f_0 contour. Thus, adding jitters to the f_0 contour is

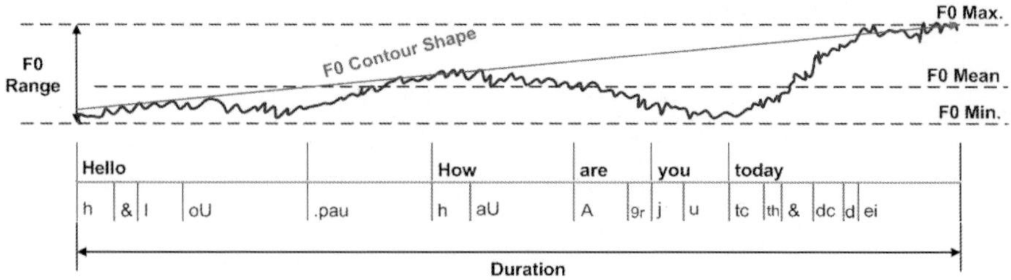

Fig. 5.9: Adding jitters is equivalent to adding noise to the f_0 contour.

essentially equivalent to adding noise to the f_0 contour, as shown in Figure 5.9. By jitter simulation we can observe voice quality change in synthetic speech to a certain (noticeable) degree.

5.3.4.4 *Diphone-based Speech Synthesis*

In diphone-based speech synthesis, small segments of recorded speech (diphones) are concatenated together to create a speech signal. These segments of speech are recorded by a human speaker in a monotonic pitch to aid the concatenation process, which is carried out by employing one of the signal processing techniques including the residual excited linear prediction (RELP) technique, the time-domain pitch synchronous overlap-add (TD-PSOLA) technique, and the multiband resynthesis pitch synchronous overlap-add (MBR-PSOLA) technique [Dutoit (1997)]. The prosody of the diphone units is also forced to match that of the desired specification at this point. It is widely admitted that diphone-based speech synthesis inevitably introduces artifacts to synthetic speech due to prosody modification. However, in order to generate expressive speech, the diphone units are subject to extreme prosody modification. In order to alleviate this difficulty, we can record the diphone database with multiple instances for every diphone. The same diphone will be recorded monotonically but at multiple pitch levels and with multiple durations. During synthesis, given a target prosody specification, we can then choose the diphone unit whose prosody parameters are the closest to those of the target. In this way we believe that we can obtain higher-quality expressive speech by reducing the amount of signal processing required for prosody matching in a diphone-based speech synthesizer.

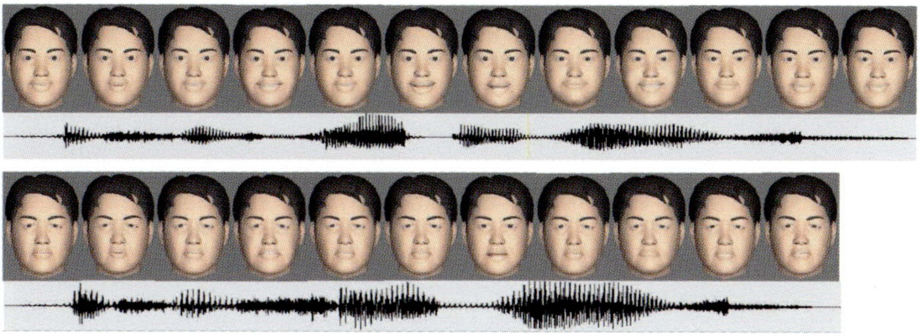

Fig. 5.10: Examples of animation of emotive audio-visual avatar with associated synthetic emotive speech waveform. (Top): The avatar says "This is happy voice." (Bottom): The avatar says "This is sad voice."

5.4 Evaluations

Based on the system framework and methods described in the previous section, we have built a 3D text-driven expressive audio-visual avatar system called EAVA [Tang *et al.* (2008b)]. We have obtained preliminary but promising experiment results for rendering neutral as well as several basic emotions: happy, joyful, sad, angry, afraid, bored, and yawning [Tang *et al.* (2008a)]. Figure 5.10 displays two examples of the results, namely, the animation sequence of facial expressions along with the associated waveforms of expressive synthetic speech generated for the happy and sad emotional states. That is, the avatar says "This is happy voice" and "This is sad voice" respectively.

We have conducted an informal evaluation on expressive synthetic speech, which shows that, for expressive speech synthesis, negative emotions (e.g., sad, angry, afraid) are more successfully synthesized than positive emotions (happy, joyful). For some emotions such as joyful and fear, artifacts are easily observed in the synthesized speech due to extreme prosody modification by signal processing. While the expressive synthetic speech alone cannot be always recognized by a listener, it can be easily distinguished when combined with compatible facial expressions.

We have also conducted a series of subjective listening experiments to evaluate the expressiveness of the EAVA system. We have derived the parameters (rate factors, gradients, etc.) for the manipulation rules that control the various aspects of the global prosody settings and voice quality from the literature and manually adjusted these parameters by listening tests. The system is capable of synthesizing eight basic emotions: neutral, happy, joyful, sad, angry, afraid, bored, and yawning. We designed and conducted three subjective listening experiments on the results generated by the system. The experiment 1 uses eight speech files corresponding to the eight distinct emotions, synthesized by the system using the same semantically neutral sentence (i.e., a number). The experiment 2 also uses eight speech files, but each of the files was synthesized using a semantically meaningful sentence appropriate for the emotion that it carries. The experiment 3 incorporates the visual channel based on experiment 1. That is, each speech file was provided with an expressive talking head showing emotional facial expressions and lip movements consistent and synchronized with the speech. The experiment 4 incorporates the visual channel based on experiment 2. That is, each speech file consists of semantically neutral sentence, semantically meaningful verbal content appropriate for the emotion, and synchronized emotional facial expressions. Twenty subjects (ten males and ten females) were asked to listen to the speech files (with the help of other channels such as verbal content and facial expressions if possible), determine the emotion for each speech file (by forced-choice), and rate his or her decision with a confidence score (1: not sure, 2: likely, 3: very likely, 4: sure, 5: very sure). The results are shown in Table 5.4. In this table, recognition rate is the ratio of the correct choices, and average score is the average confidence score computed for the correct choices.

It is obviously shown in the results of the subjective listening experiments that our system has achieved a certain degree of expressiveness despite of the relatively poor performance of the prosody prediction model. As can be clearly seen, negative emotions (e.g., sad, afraid, angry) are more successfully synthesized than positive emotions (e.g., happy). This observation is consistent with what has been found in the literature. In addition, we found that the emotional states "happy" and "joyful" are often mistaken for each other. So are "afraid" and "angry" as well as "bored" and "yawning." By incorporating other channels that convey emotions such as verbal content and facial expressions, the perception of emotional affect in synthetic speech can be significantly improved.

Table 5.4: Results of subjective listening experiments. $R \longleftrightarrow$ Recognition Rate. $S \longleftrightarrow$ Average Confidence Score. Experiment 1 $\longleftrightarrow$ Speech only. Experiment 2 $\longleftrightarrow$ Speech + verbal content. Experiment 3 $\longleftrightarrow$ Speech + facial expression. Experiment 4 $\longleftrightarrow$ Speech + verbal content + facial expression.

Emotion	Experiment 1		Experiment 2		Experiment 3		Experiment 4	
	R	S	R	S	R	S	R	S
neutral	54.54%	2.83	100%	4.36	90.90%	4.1	100%	4.81
happy	18.18%	2.5	63.63%	4.57	63.63%	4.43	54.54%	4.5
joyful	45.45%	2.8	63.63%	4.86	63.63%	4.29	45.45%	5
sad	36.36%	2.75	81.81%	4.67	100%	4.18	100%	4.81
angry	18.18%	2	90.90%	4.3	90.90%	4	100%	4.63
afraid	45.45%	2.4	81.81%	4.89	72.72%	4	81.81%	5
bored	45.45%	3	81.81%	4.44	–	–	–	–
yawning	18.18%	3.5	72.72%	3.75	–	–	–	–

5.5 Conclusions and Future Work

This chapter describes the system framework and methods leading to a 3D text-driven expressive audio-visual avatar system EAVA. The three key research issues are how to synthesize natural-sounding expressive speech, how to animate realistic-looking facial expressions, and how to combine lip motion with facial expressions in a natural and realistic fashion. In particular, we propose a general framework for expressive speech synthesis using a diphone-based speech synthesizer and a differential approach. The EAVA system is capable of synthesizing eight basic emotions (i.e., neutral, happy, joyful, sad, angry, afraid, bored, and yawning), which can be readily extended. The results of subjective listening experiments indicate that a certain degree of expressiveness has been achieved by the system. There are various channels that convey emotions in daily communication. The perception of emotional affect from synthetic speech can be highly complemented by other channels such as verbal content and facial expressions.

Continuous improvements are being made to the system. In particular, our ongoing work is to pursue various data-driven methodologies in resolving the different but related aspects of this research. Potential improvements to the current system can be made within the general framework presented in this chapter by using statistical prosody prediction models instead of prosody manipulation rules, by using several diphone databases of different vocal efforts, and by using a multipitch multiduration diphone database. It is believed that after the incorporation of all these factors, the quality (intelligibility, naturalness and expressiveness) of the expressive synthetic speech can be further dramatically improved. The success of this research will advance significantly the state-of-the-art of both human-computer interaction and human–human communication.

Chapter 6

Model Based Video Encoding

6.1 Introduction

For transferring instructor's appearance and motion to the learners' side, a generic video encoding paradigm is usually used in current online learning systems. However, considering the particular characteristics of teaching videos, the generic encoding schemes are not efficient and robust to the variety of network and device quality of learners' side. Customizing video encoding for distance learning using animation of 3D face models is a promising direction to this demand.

The variety of available facial animation techniques provides a broad range of virtual character animation graphics quality. The more detailed models usually provide better rendering but in the meantime require more careful design, human labeling label and computing resources. In this chapter, we introduce a face model generated from the 3D model reconstructed from 2D images and controlled by 3D tracking from 2D videos. The motion parameters recovered from real time tracking are represented as MPEG4 FAPs. These parameters can be used to play any facial animation rigs that are MPEG-4 compliant. We compare the avatar animation performance with another system of the same modality and show that our system achieves higher quality both visually and quantitatively and suitable for interactive remote education experience.

6.2 Animation Model Construction

The avatar is at the center of our facial animation rig. It consists of a fully textured 3D mesh with 8955 vertices in correspondence and a set of FAP definition tables. Each table includes the unit movements applied to the related vertices. In this section, we will examine the structure and procedure for building these two components.

Shape and texture model. We use the algorithm described in Chapter 3 for recovering shape and texture from a frame of the video. This process can be done at the beginning of the session or can be done offline. The detailed mesh with full texture is stored at local site or transferred to remote site before the tracking session starts.

Motion model. Designing the motion model for 3D models has been an important task for building functioning avatar. The blendshape based presentation is the most widely used motion model [Pighin and Lewis (2006)]. The model synthesizes the movement of all the vertices in the mesh as a linear combination of a basis of fundamental movements. In these models, constructing the new deformed version of the model is reduced to finding the blendshape parameters. The most common methods of building blendshape rigs are using Facial Action Coding System (FACS) and MPEG-4's Facial Animation Parameters (FAPs).

These blendshape rigs are normally created by two methods, either trained from groundtruth data or from manual design. In our system, the blendshapes are designed following FAPs standard and are created using both manual design and data interpolation. The unit deformation are manually created on the sparse set of feature points, then interpolated for other vertices of the mesh following the method described in [Jiang *et al.* (2002)].

Illustrations of some of the FAPs movement of original feature points and interpolated on mesh's vertices are shown in Figure 6.1.

6.3 Performance-driven Animations

The avatar with the geometry and motion model constructed can be played by multiple source of controlling factors, such as text, speech, emotion or performance. In this section, we will introduce our performance driven avatar. In the performance driven avatar application, we analyze the video frame and estimate the facial motion represented by FAP values. These FAP values can be used to control any compatible face model to generate facial animation that resembles the facial actions of a performer in the video. The deformed face are recovered by using Eq. 3.11. The workflow of the performance driven avatar algorithm with visual examples is shown in Figure 6.2.

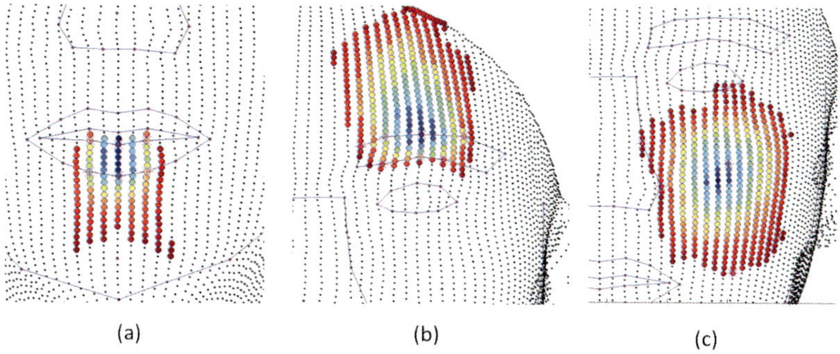

Fig. 6.1: Examples of Facial animation table of some FAPs. (a): FAP5 "Raise_b_midlip," (b): FAP33 "Raise_l_m_eyebrow," (c): FAP39 "Puff_l_cheek". Color of circles indicates the intensity of motion applied on the specific location when the FAP is activated. Stars are the feature points affected by the FAP.

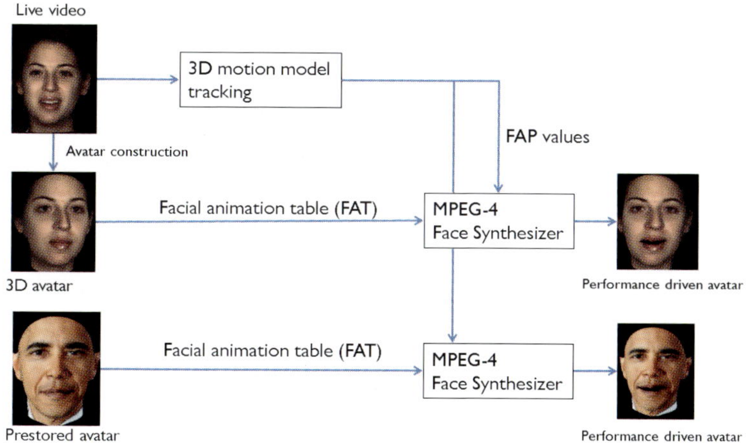

Fig. 6.2: Performance-driven avatars workflow.

In the case the rendered avatar is of the performer, the system will be acting as a video encoding and decoding system. The avatar can also be of another subject or a cartoon character. In that case we have a performance driven animation.

6.4 3D Model-based Video Coding

The performance driven avatar can be used as the core engine for the 3D model based video coding paradigm. At the transmitting end, the facial motions from tracking are regulated into MPEG4's FAPs. When transmitted to the receiving end, these parameters are used to play the speaker's avatar. This paradigm forms a video coding system with very high compression ratio. Potentially, the avatar can be edited for aesthetic purposes. Also, its motion can be adjusted for video stabilization or gaze modification.

Specifically, consider the scenario of asymmetrical teleconference, where one stationary end with multiple users and several mobile ends with single users are communicating with each other. Extension to multiple stationary sties can be made by integration with an existing symmetric teleconference system. At the stationary end, the active speaker is first detected; and the identity/face/expression of the speaker is robustly extracted using both intensity and depth cameras. The extracted information, which is essential to convey a feeling of in-person conversation, can be transmitted to mobile ends in the form of the parameters of a speaker appearance model. At the mobile end, the received information can be used to render an avatar of the current speaker.

6.5 Experimental Results

We use the pose angles and FAP values to play another pre-built avatar named 'Obama'. Examples of these results are shown in Figure 6.3. We compare the results of our system with those of a tracking algorithm based on Piecewise Bézier volume (PBVD) [Tu *et al.* (2003)]. The comparison shows that the quality of our avatar rendering is visually significantly better in both stability and image quality. Some examples of the comparison are shown in Figure 6.4.

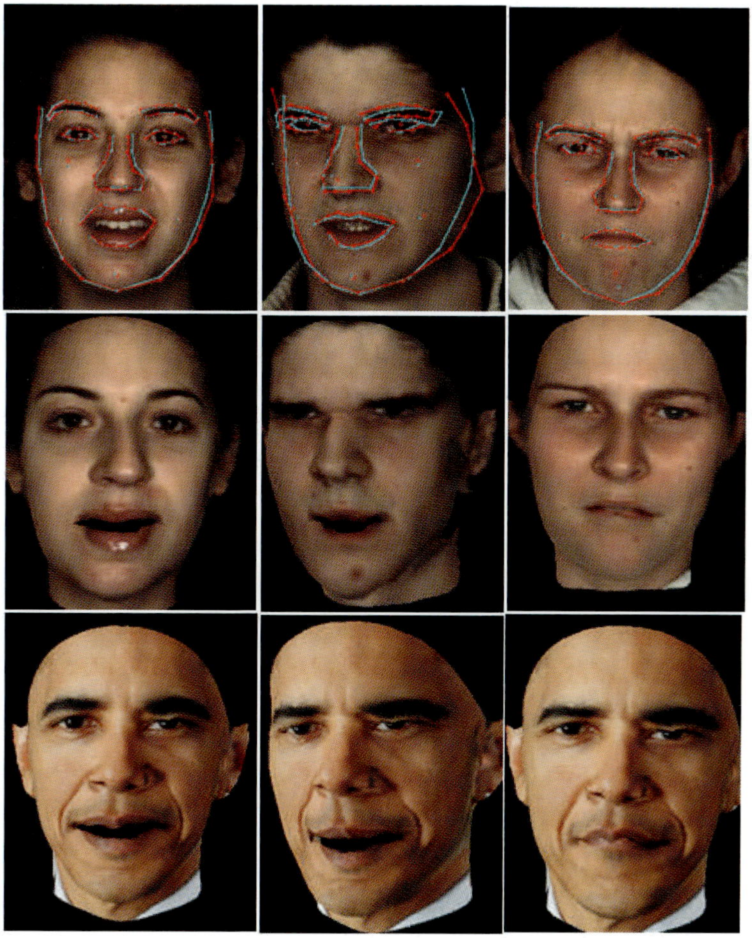

Fig. 6.3: Examples of performance driven avatar. First row: input video frame with tracked landmarks; red: visually tracking result, cyan: model fitted result. Second row: rendering of the subject's avatar. Third row: rendering of the 'Obama' avatar.

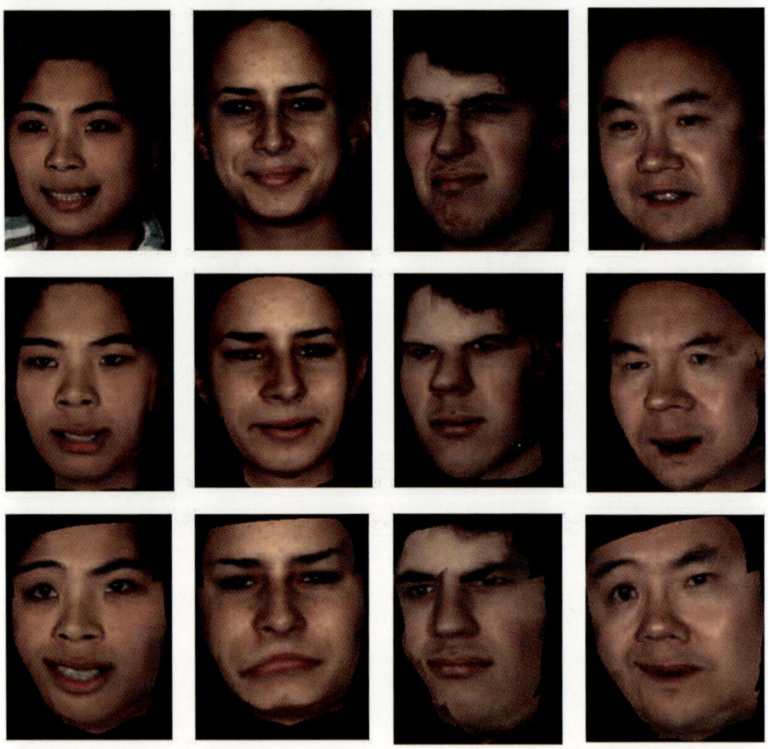

Fig. 6.4: Comparison of avatar quality on some examples. First row: input frames. Second row: our avatar rendering. Third row: PBVD [Tu *et al.* (2003)] avatar rendering.

Chapter 7

Student Engagement Monitoring

7.1 Introduction

A recent revolution in the world of education has occurred in the form of MOOCs: Massively Open Online Courses. These courses, offered by services such as Coursera, EdX, Udacity and others, provide asynchronous, remote instruction to large numbers of students, often numbering in the tens of thousands. While such courses build strong online communities, there is often a lack of direct communication between the students and the instructor. Lectures are delivered as prerecorded video which means that the instructor misses out on the real-time classroom activity and feedback. This makes it far more difficult for instructors to determine if their students are following the course material. Furthermore, college class sizes are continually growing. This has led to larger class sizes with hundreds of students thereby hindering the ability of an instructor to perceive the attentiveness of the entire class.

In this chapter, we present a student monitoring system, presented in part in [Khorrami *et al.* (2014)], that uses ordinary RGB cameras to measure the engagement of students as they observe online material, either remotely in a MOOC or locally in a large class. To accomplish this, we model student engagement by using a rough estimate of their eye gaze position to determine if the student is paying attention to the course material displayed on the computer screen. We model the approximation of the student's gaze using the 3D face model tracker and the gaze estimator presented in Chapters 3 and 4. The gaze point can also be tracked over time and correlated with the subject material to determine what particular sections of the lecture drew the most interest. Our proposed system can also be used to assess the affective state of the students during a lecture by analyzing their facial expressions and relaying them to the instructor. We accomplish by adapting the method presented in [Tariq *et al.* (2012a)] and Chapter 2 to the educational setting.

The remainder of this chapter is organized as follows. Section 7.2 surveys the related work with regards to monitoring systems in educational environments. Section 7.3 presents the basic framework of our proposed non-invasive student monitoring system. Section 7.4 describes how the gaze point computed using the algorithm described in Chapter 4, can be used to quantify attention. We also discuss how the system uses facial expression recognition as an alternate way to assess a student's level of engagement. Section 7.5 describes how the system is deployed and how the resulting classroom engagement statistics are presented to the instructor. We also present some preliminary experiments on attention classification based on the gaze point approximations. Section 7.6 summarizes our system's contributions and provides directions for future research.

7.2 Related Work

Current student monitoring systems are designed such that an instructor is able to gather and capture data on how their students are progressing in the class even when one-on-one interaction is impossible. However, the manner in which monitoring systems can go about collecting this data is vastly different and can be divided into two categories: indirect monitoring and direct monitoring.

The most common types of *indirect monitoring systems* use Course Management Systems (CMS) or Learning Management Systems (LMS) to collect their data. These constructs allow instructors to do a variety of tasks with regards to their course such as posting homeworks, administering quizzes and managing discussion forums. CMSs are used extensively by universities through services like Moodle [Dougiamas (2002)] while monitoring systems such as CourseVis [Mazza and Dimitrova (2007)], MonSys [Martins *et al.* (2012)], and MATEP [Zorrilla and Álvarez (2008)] have been designed to collect data specifically from CMSs using logs of student activities such as login times, forum activity, exam grades etc. This type of monitoring is considered indirect because the data is collected offline and only includes coarse metadata of the learning session. While these indirect techniques are non-invasive and do not require sophisticated machinery, they are unable to model what occurs in real-time during a lecture and the collected metadata only provides weak clues of the students' behavior. Work by Avouris *et al.* [Avouris *et al.* (2005)] tried to augment the data contained in log files with media taken during classroom sessions, however designing such a system would probably be infeasible for the large scale online learning paradigm.

In contrast, *direct monitoring systems* provide instructors with the ability to see exactly what their students are doing during a lecture. Products like Smart Sync [Sync (2011)], Stoneware [Stoneware (2011)], and Netop Vision [Netop (2013)] provide instructors with access to a student's screen, as well as the ability to disable web browsing and even see what programs the student is running in the background. While this may be useful in primary or secondary school settings, such access would be considered intrusive in higher education settings or MOOCs. Therefore, it is necessary to develop a protocol where an instructor can infer the attentiveness of their students without explicit intervention.

In this work, we propose a real-time student monitoring system that provides an in-depth description of each student in the classroom without being intrusive. While we use webcams to acquire data from each of the students, we do not transmit the raw video data to the instructor. Instead, we define a protocol to represent the visual data in a more abstract yet descriptive manner. Thus, our method is able to combine the positive aspects of both *direct* and *indirect monitoring systems* while simultaneously avoiding their negative aspects.

7.3 System Overview

Our system models a classroom using the client-server model in computer networking, where the clients represent the students and the server represents the instructor. A visualization of our system is provided in Figure 7.1. On the student side, each subject accesses course material using their local machines while our software collects information such as the facial feature points and head pose direction or the student's affective state using a webcam and transmits them to the server.

The server then uses the incoming data from the clients to estimate the subject's level of engagement while also performing real-time data visualization and offline data aggregation. Online data aggregation uses visualization controls to provide the instructor with a concise representation of each student's state in relation to others in the class while offline data

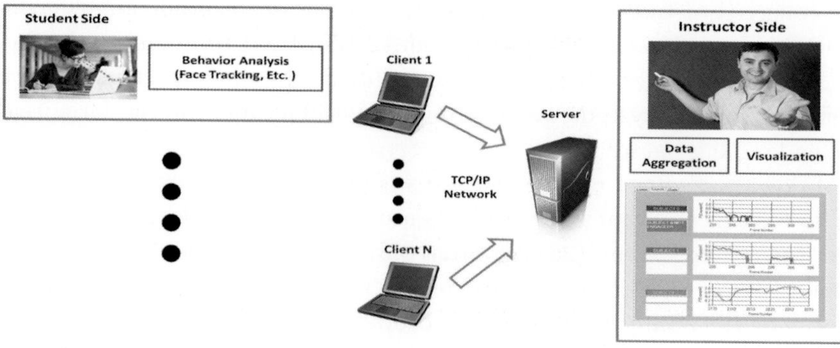

Fig. 7.1: Student Monitoring System Layout. Each client (left) extracts behavioral information from each student using face tracking or facial expression recognition and transmits the data over TCP/IP to a central server (right). The server collects the data from each subject and plots attention charts for the instructor to view in real-time. Images displayed were obtained courtesy of [Alexander Raths/Shutterstock] and [Zhang Bao/Getty Images].

aggregation maintains a running log of all client activity and displays holistic information about the entire session.

7.4 Engagement Estimation

7.4.1 *Gaze Direction*

While engagement/attention seems to be a difficult concept to model mathematically, there exist informative cues that can be used to infer the attention level of an audience. One very natural cue is a person's gaze. In particular, the location of a person's gaze focus and the duration for which they maintain their focus are useful indicators of attention. Our decision to use eye gaze was inspired by the work of Just *et al.* [Just and Carpenter (1976)], which indicated that the duration of a person's eye fixations is directly related to the amount of neural processing power they are devoting to a particular task, which can then be directly related to a person's attention level. There have also been recent studies conducted by Rose *et al.* [Rose *et al.* (2013)] and by Underwood *et al.* [Underwood *et al.* (2003)] that have used fixations/looking times as cues to model attention with reasonable success.

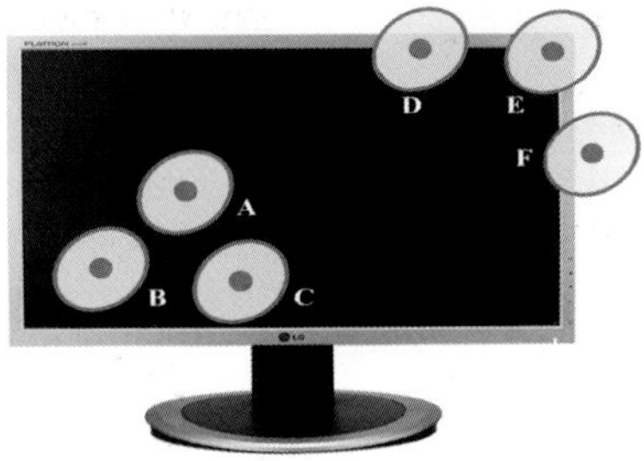

Fig. 7.2: Illustration of how our system computes the attention confidence score for different gaze points. The amount each point overlaps with the screen is denoted by the shaded green region. Points A, B, and C have full overlap and therefore, correspond to points with high attention confidence scores, while points D, E, and F have partial overlap resulting in lower confidence scores. Best viewed in color.

We compute each subject's point of gaze using the technique described in [Khorrami *et al.* (2014)] and Chapter 4. The algorithm first uses 3D face model tracking to estimate the position of the subject's head in 3D and then uses the estimated head pose parameters to define the gaze direction. After estimating the location of the subject's gaze, our algorithms verifies the point is within the monitor's dimensions in the world coordinate system. We develop a confidence score to better quantify a user's level of engagement. The confidence score is derived by centering a Gaussian distribution over each client's gaze point and computing the area of intersection between the Gaussian and the screen. Thus, if the user's gaze point is well within the monitor's dimensions then the confidence score will be high. Similarly, if the user's gaze point is completely outside the monitor's dimensions, the score will go to zero. This idea is visualized in Figure 7.2. If a student's confidence score remains zero for an extended period of time, then the interface signals the instructor that the student has become disengaged. The parameters of the Gaussian were computed by observing the gaze behavior of 10 subjects as they followed a generated set of patterns displayed on the computer screen.

7.4.2 *Emotion Recognition*

While gaze estimation efficiently conveys the level of the attention of the students, the affective state of the subjects is also an important form of

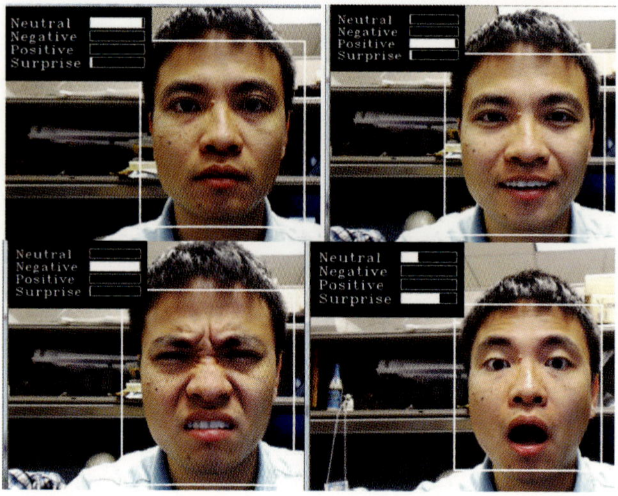

Fig. 7.3: Examples of video frames being classified into four types of expressions by our algorithm.

feedback for the instructor. One of the most effective and important cues for emotion recognition is facial expressions. To exploit this cue, we apply the method for non-frontal expression recognition described in [Tariq *et al.* (2012a)].

Most existing works focus on recognizing the six canonical expressions: anger, fear, disgust, sad, happy and surprise. Although these expressions are universal and recognizable across different cultures [Ekman (1971)], in most applications, having six measurements is not optimal for reviewing or evaluating the attitude of the subject. In our implementation, we choose to classify four types of expression: Positive, Negative, Surprise and Neutral. A screen capture of four types of expressions being recognized on an example video is shown in Figure 7.3.

At the client side, the facial images from the video frames are used to recognize the expression class among the four aforementioned categories. The results include the likelihoods that the facial image belongs to each of the four classes. They together with metadata fields form a package for each frame and is sent to server. At the server, the result is aggregated to form stacked bar graph to show to the instructor.

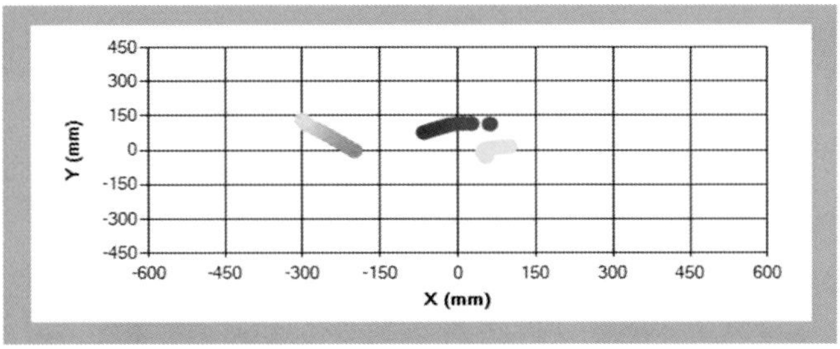

Fig. 7.4: Screen area visualization showing gaze points of multiple students on a coordinate grid. Each color corresponds to gaze points of a different student. The weight of each gaze point represents the server's confidence score (darker → more confident). This figure is best viewed in color.

7.5 Experiments

7.5.1 *Qualitative Evaluation*

Our class monitoring system allows for the simultaneous monitoring of the engagement levels of multiple students in a given classroom session. For our qualitative experiments, we simulate an online course environment by having three clients connect to the server where each client is equipped with a computer and a Logitech c920 webcam. Each client runs an instance of the face tracking code locally which extracts their eye locations and head pose angles. A packet is constructed using the x, y locations of the left and right eyes, and the head pose angles and is transmitted to the server via TCP/IP. The server uses the geometrical model described in Chapter 4 to estimate the gaze point location of each client and displays them on a common screen like the one shown in Figure 7.4. Each sequence of colored dots corresponds to a different student's gaze trace. The server also computes the gaze confidence score for each subject over time and displays the curves to the instructor. An example of these curves is shown in Figure 7.5.

When analyzing the emotional state of multiple subjects, we execute the following setup. Each client runs the emotion recognition algorithm described previously. The algorithm outputs four emotion confidence scores corresponding to how neutral, positive, negative, or surprised the user appears and transmits them to the server.

At every time instance and for every client, the server takes the vector S defined by the emotion confidence scores and computes a normalized version of the vector, S', such that all of the values in S' sum to 1. In essence, the

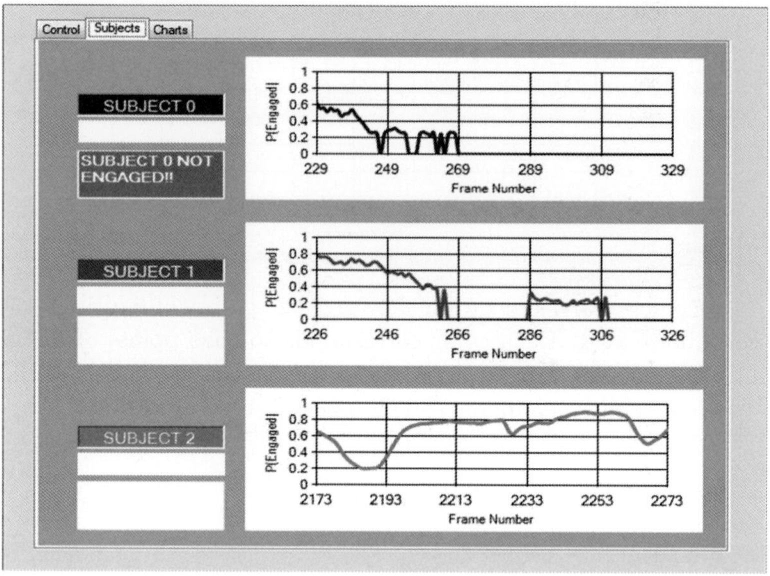

Fig. 7.5: Sample server display for simulated classroom session. Each curve plots the engagement confidence score of each subject over time. This figure is best viewed in color.

scores are modeled as a probability distribution in order to better ascertain a subject's affective state. The normalized scores are stored and logged for every subject and displayed using a stacked column chart. Figure 7.6 provides an example displaying the states of three subjects. In each of the stacked column charts, the four colors represent the four possible emotional states of the user (green: neutral, red: negative, blue: positive, magenta: surprise). We see that the first subject is initially negative but changes their expression to being surprised, while the second and three subjects are predominantly positive and negative respectively.

7.5.2 *Quantitative Evaluation*

To directly measure the accuracy of our gaze system in estimating engagement, we design a second experiment to detect whether a student is paying attention or they are distracted. With regards to our setup, these two states map to looking at the screen and looking off the screen, respectively. We simulate the scenario where a student is looking at a laptop screen displaying lecture material. To accommodate this experiment, the laptop screen

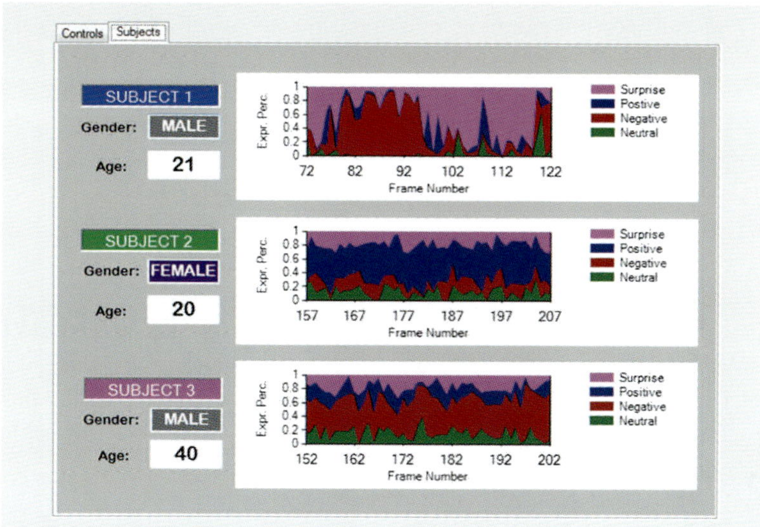

Fig. 7.6: Simultaneous visualization of the affective states of three clients over time. Each client's affective state is represented as a probability distribution over time and is displayed using a stacked bar chart. This figure is best viewed in color.

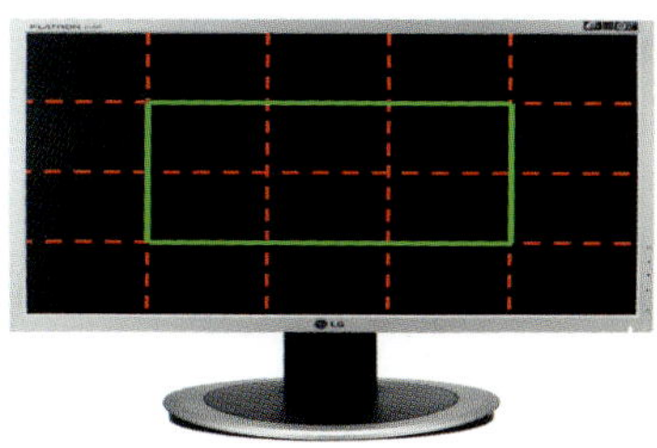

Fig. 7.7: Rectangular grid used when computing engagement accuracy. Screen is broken up into 4x5 grid. Blocks within the inner 2×3 grid are labeled 1 while blocks outside are labeled 0.

area is synthesized by inscribing a rectangle on a larger desktop screen as shown in Figure 7.7. In this setup, the 2×3 grid of blocks within the inscribed rectangle contains the positive samples and the blocks outside are considered the negative samples. Once again, a subject is instructed to look at each block as it is highlighted on the screen and our system computes the estimated gaze point to determine whether the user is looking at

Table 7.1: Subject engagement classification accuracy computed for all 4 test subjects

Subject	Engagement Classification Accuracy
1	85%
2	70%
3	75%
4	80%
Average	75%

the laptop screen. This prediction is then compared with the ground truth label. We compute the accuracy across all of the blocks for 4 subjects and present the results in Table 7.1. Indeed, the subjects' gaze points allows us to determine whether the engagement of a given subject with an accuracy of about 75%.

7.6 Conclusions and Future Work

We have shown that an ordinary webcam can find and follow head pose well enough in real-time to determine whether a subject is engaged with an accuracy of 75%. Our statistics on gaze estimation are preliminary but prove the concept that a webcam can be used to estimate student gaze on coarse sections of the screen. We also demonstrated that our system is able to capture the affective state of multiple students and use that to convey the overall mood of the classroom to the instructor over time.

The next steps for future research would be to find other cues that can be used to give a more complete summarization of a classroom session such as age and demographic information. However, in order to truly close the gap between effective teaching and learning, this system would need to be studied further in a formal educational experimental setting.

Chapter 8

Conclusion and Future Work

In this book, we have investigated a collection of facial processing techniques for analyzing and synthesizing static and dynamic geometry of human faces. The collection includes appearance based expression recognition, feature based 3D morphable model fitting, 3D motion tracking, avatar playing and eye gaze recognition. The quantitative evaluation of the experiments shows that the algorithms and based-upon systems are competent for state-of-the-art quality for human faces and facial behaviors analysis. The efficiency of the algorithms has been demonstrated to be suitable for real time applications.

We also investigate the applications of the facial processing techniques on building core features for interactive distance learning systems. For lecture delivery, we proposed to use 3D model based avatar for very low bit rate video encoding of lecturer's facial appearance. In the feedback direction, the expression recognition and eye gaze direction algorithms were integrated into a realtime remote monitoring of students' engagement during distant learning sessions. The demonstration modules have been built and experimented in simulated environment. The qualitative and quantitative evaluation results proved that the techniques can readily be applied in both massive open coursewares or private webinar style distance learning setups.

From the investigation, we also pointed out that facial structure and motion analysis and synthesis are still challenging problems. The sources of the difficulties include specific irregular characteristics of the human face shapes, the volatile and subtle nature of the human behavior and the diversity of the imaging environment. To address these challenges, we propose several directions to improve the robustness, accuracy, and efficiency of the system including using robust features for visual tracking, exploiting depth signal for model fitting and tracking, and adapting the framework into a client-cloud architecture.

8.1 Robust Visual Tracking and Motion Model

In the 3D model tracking algorithm introduced in Chapter 3, we use the classical Lucas–Kanade optical flow algorithm with multi-resolution pyramid scheme. This method is employed for its fast implementation, simplicity and the adequate performance in a studio environment. However, in realistic scenarios, with difficult environment conditions of lighting, background, and noise, we would need more robust visual tracking remedies, such as using invariant robust features.

In recent years, SIFT-like features such as SIFT [Liu *et al.* (2011)], SURF [Bay *et al.* (2006)], FAST [Rosten and Drummond (2005)], and other invariant appearance features draw enormous amount of attention for their robustness to changes of the scene like pose, scale and direction. These robust features usually come with detection of interest points which consist of more texture for more reliable tracking.

Besides the visual tracking feature, the deformation model can also be improved by being regularized with a set of dynamic constraints on the model's parameters. In the current system, the model is constrained by a set of heuristic rules, which set hard thresholds for the parameters. Although simple, this method possesses limitations in its inability to handle strong natural expressions and sometimes allows exaggerated facial movements. In the new model, these thresholds will be learned by analyzing real training expressive facial 3D videos. The correlations between thresholds of different parameters will also be explored. These improvements are expected to help smooth and regularize the motion model for more natural expressive face synthesis.

8.2 Client-cloud Architecture

In this future work, we propose to adapt our face tracking and avatar system into cloud computing infrastructure. The framework effectively uses a 3D model to do very low bit rate video compression using cloud computing setup which includes a number of mobile devices with low computing capability connected to cloud servers with GPUs and a multicore CPUs. At the client device of the performer, the raw facial video (either RGB or RGBD)

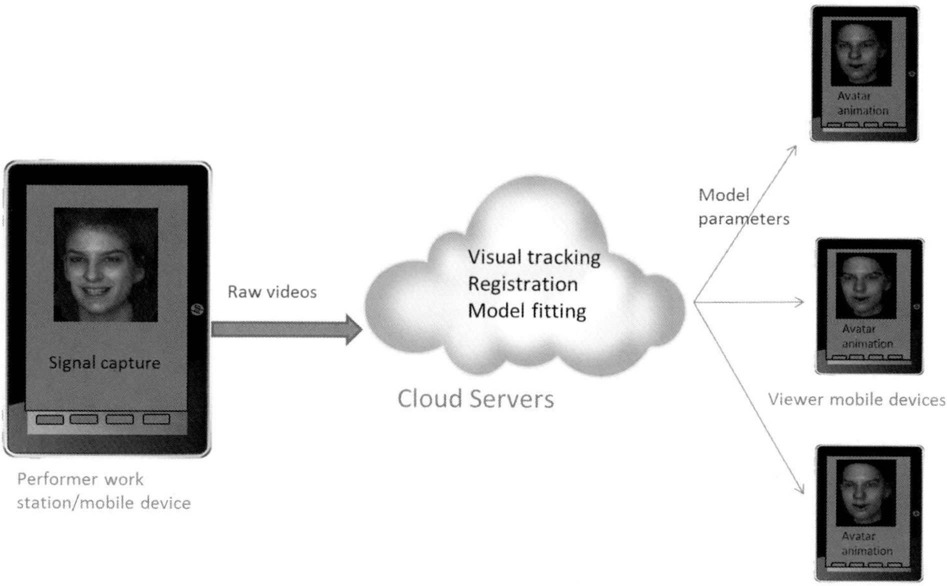

Fig. 8.1: Illustration of the face tracking and video coding using client-cloud architecture.

is captured and transferred to the server for processing. At the server side, the compressed RGB and depth videos are decoded and may need to be synchronized. They are then used to fit the shape and motion model. The parameters that result from tracking will then be transferred to the client devices at other sites for avatar rendering. The workflow of this approach is depicted in Figure 8.1.

8.3 Residual Compensation for Photorealistic Video Coding

In most telepresence applications, a faithful reconstruction of facial video is crucial for user satisfaction. With the current avatar rendering in Chapter 5, the level of accuracy may be limited due to system imperfections, particularly in difficult environmental conditions such as extreme poses, strong expression or harsh lighting. In order to compensate for this inaccuracy, we propose to recover the authentic representation of the image by computing the residual of the original video frame compared to the rendered

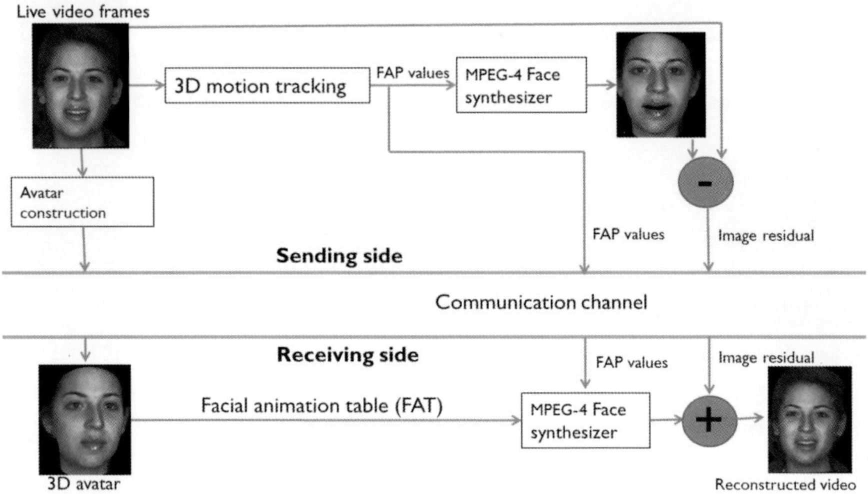

Fig. 8.2: Model-based video coding framework. Image residual are extracted at the sending side and is added up to model rendered image at the receiving side.

avatar image at the source. This residual is transmitted to the receiving end and added to the synthesized image to get the perfect reconstruction. The framework is illustrated in Figure 8.2.

In this scenario, the number of bits needed to represent the residual determines the efficiency of the video coding system. This depends on the energy of the residual signal which, in our experiments, is affected the most by two factors: the misalignment caused by the global tracking error and the change in lighting conditions. To reduce the size of the residual, we propose to reduce these effects by applying post-processing steps on the synthesized images. Firstly, the rendered avatar is registered with the original face using 2D registration techniques. After that the lighting on the avatar's image is normalized with the original by a 2D illumination compensation method.

When the image is ready, the minimized residual is computed between the original and the rendered images and is compressed by regular video codecs and transmitted through the data network. Compared to the motion model parameters, the residual has a data size of higher order and therefore will be more susceptible to networking issues such as latency, jitter, and packet loss.

Bibliography

Ambady, N. and Rosenthal, R. (1992). Thin slices of expressive behavior as predictors of interpersonal consequences: A meta-analysis, *Psychological Bulletin* **111**, 2, pp. 256–274.

Anderson, K. and McOwan, P. W. (2006). A real-time automated system for the recognition of human facial expressions, *IEEE Transactions on Systems, Man, and Cybernetics, Part B: Cybernetics* **36**, 1, pp. 96–105.

Arun, K. S., Huang, T. S., and Blostein, S. D. (1987). Least-squares fitting of two 3-d point sets, *IEEE Transactions on Pattern Analysis Machine and Intelligence* **9**, 5, pp. 698–700.

Asteriadis, S., Soufleros, D., Karpouzis, K., and Kollias, S. (2009). A natural head pose and eye gaze dataset, in *Proceedings of the International Workshop on Affective-Aware Virtual Agents and Social Robots* (ACM), p. 1.

Avouris, N., Komis, V., Fiotakis, G., Margaritis, M., and Voyiatzaki, E. (2005). Logging of fingertip actions is not enough for analysis of learning activities, in *AIED'05 Workshop on Usage Analysis in Learning Systems*, pp. 1–8.

Baluja, S. and Pomerleau, D. (1994). Non-intrusive gaze tracking using artificial neural networks, Tech. rep., DTIC Document.

Bartlett, M. S., Littlewort, G., Braathen, P., Sejnowski, T. J., and Movellan, J. R. (2003). A prototype for automatic recognition of spontaneous facial actions, in *Advances in Neural Information Processing Systems*, Vol. 15, pp. 1271–1278.

Bay, H., Tuytelaars, T., and Van Gool, L. (2006). Surf: Speeded up robust features, in *Computer Vision — ECCV 2006*, pp. 404–417.

Beeler, T., Bickel, B., Beardsley, P., Sumner, B., and Gross, M. (2010). High-quality single-shot capture of facial geometry, *ACM Transactions on Graphics (Proceedings of SIGGRAPH)* **29**, 3, pp. 40:1–40:9.

Belhumeur, P. N., Hespanha, J. P., and Kriegman, D. J. (1997). Eigenfaces vs. fisherfaces: Recognition using class specific linear projection, *IEEE Transactions on Pattern Analysis and Machine Intelligence* **19**, 7, pp. 711–720.

Berretti, S., Del Bimbo, A., Pala, P., Amor, B. B., and Daoudi, M. (2010). A set of selected sift features for 3d facial expression recognition, in *Proceedings of International Conference on Pattern Recognition*, pp. 4125–4128.

Beymer, D. and Flickner, M. (2003). Eye gaze tracking using an active stereo head, in *IEEE Computer Society Conference on Computer Vision and Pattern Recognition, 2003*, Vol. 2 (IEEE), pp. II–451.

Bishop, C. (2006). *Pattern Recognition and Machine Learning* (Springer).

Biswas, S., Aggarwal, G., and Chellappa, R. (2009). Robust estimation of albedo for illumination-invariant matching and shape recovery, *IEEE Transactions on Pattern Analysis and Machine Intelligence* **31**, 5, pp. 884–899.

Blanz, V. and Vetter, T. (1999). A morphable model for the synthesis of 3d faces, in *Proceedings of the 26th Annual Conference on Computer graphics and interactive techniques, SIGGRAPH'99* (ACM Press/Addison-Wesley Publishing Co., New York, NY, USA), pp. 187–194.

Blanz, V. and Vetter, T. (2003). Face recognition based on fitting a 3D morphable model, *IEEE Transactions on Pattern Analysis and Machine Intelligence* **25**, 9, pp. 1063–1074.

Boureau, Y.-L., Bach, F., LeCun, Y., and Ponce, J. (2010). Learning mid-level features for recognition, in *IEEE Conference on Computer Vision and Pattern Recognition*.

Bradley, D., Heidrich, W., Popa, T., and Sheffer, A. (2010). High resolution passive facial performance capture, *ACM Transactions on Graphics* **29**, 4, pp. 41:1–41:10.

Brolly, X. L. and Mulligan, J. B. (2004). Implicit calibration of a remote gaze tracker, in *Conference on Computer Vision and Pattern Recognition Workshop, 2004. CVPRW'04* (IEEE), pp. 134–134.

Burkhardt, F. (2000). *Simulation emotionaler sprechweise mit sprachsyntheseverfahren*, Ph.D thesis, TU Berlin.

Burkhardt, F. (2005). Emofilt: the simulation of emotional speech by prosody-transformation, in *Proceedings on INTERSPEECH-2005*, pp. 509–512.

Cahn, J. E. (1989). *Generating expression in synthesized speech*, Master's thesis, MIT Media Lab.

Cao, Y., Faloutsos, P., and Pighin, F. (2005). Expressive speech-driven facial animation, *ACM Transactions on Graph* **24**, 4.

Cao, Z., Yin, Q., Tang, X., and Sun, J. (2010). Face recognition with learning-based descriptor, in *IEEE Conference on Computer Vision and Pattern Recognition (CVPR), 2010* (IEEE), pp. 2707–2714.

Chang, Y., Hu, C., Feris, R., and Turk, M. (2006). Manifold based analysis of facial expression, *Image and Vision Computing* **24**, 6, pp. 605–614.

Cootes, T., Edwards, G. J., and Taylor, C. J. (2001). Active appearance models, *IEEE Transactions on PAMI* **23**, pp. 681–685.

Cootes, T. F., Taylor, C. J., Cooper, D. H., and Graham, J. (1995). Active shape models-their training and application, *Computer Vision and Image Understanding* **61**, 1, pp. 38–59.

Corive, R., Douglas-Cowie, E., Tsapatsoulis, N., Votsis, G., Kollias, S., Fellenz, W., and Taylor, J. G. (2001). Emotion recognition in human–computer interaction, *IEEE Signal Processing Magazine* **18**, 1, pp. 32–80.

Cristinacce, D., Cootes, T., and Scott, I. (2004). A multi-stage approach to facial feature detection, in *BMVC*, pp. 231–240.

Dhall, A., Asthana, A., Goecke, R., and Gedeon, T. (2011). Emotion recognition using phog and lpq features, in *2011 IEEE International Conference on Automatic Face Gesture Recognition and Workshops (FG 2011)*, pp. 878–883.

Dougiamas, M. (2002). Modular object-oriented dynamic learning environment (moodle), `https://moodle.org/`.

Dutoit, T. (1997). *An Introduction to Text-to-Speech Synthesis* (Kluwer Academic Publishers, Dordrecht).

Ekman, P. (1971). Universals and cultural differences in facial expressions of emotion, in *Nebraska Symposium on Motivation* (University of Nebraska Press).

Ekman, P. (1993). *Facial Action Coding System: Manual* (Consulting Psychologists Press).

Ekman, P. and Friesen, W. V. (1977). *The Facial Action Coding System* (Consulting Psychological Press, Palo Alto, Calif.).

Ekman, P., Friesen, W. V., O'Sullivan, M., Chan, A., Diacoyanni-Tarlatzis, I., Heider, K., Krause, R., LeCompte, W. A., Pitcairn, T., Ricci-Bitti, P. E., Scherer, K., Tomita, M., and Tzavaras, A. (1987). Universals and cultural differences in the judgments of facial expressions of emotion, *Journal of Personality and Social Psychology* **53**, 4, pp. 712–717.

Ekman, P., Huang, T. S., Sejnowski, T., and Hager, J. (1993). Final report to nsf of the planning workshop on facial expression understanding, *Available from HIL-0*.

Fan, R.-E., Chang, K.-W., Hsieh, C.-J., Wang, X.-R., and Lin, C.-J. (2008). LIBLINEAR: A library for large linear classification, *Journal of Machine Learning Research* **9**, pp. 1871–1874.

Fei-Fei, L., Fergus, R., and Perona, P. (2007). Learning generative visual models from few training examples: An incremental Bayesian approach tested on 101 object categories, *Computer Vision and Image Understanding* **106**, 1, pp. 59–70.

Forsyth, D. A. and Ponce, J. (2002). *Computer Vision: A Modern Approach* (Prentice-Hall Professional Technical Reference).

Fu, Y., Tang, H., Tu, J., Tao, H., and Huang, T. S. (2010). Human-centered face computing in multimedia interaction and communication, in *Intelligent Multimedia Communication: Techniques and Applications* (Springer, Berlin), pp. 465–505.

Fu, Y. and Zheng, N. (2006). M-face: An appearance-based photorealistic model for multiple facial attributes rendering, *IEEE Transactions on CSVT* **16**, 7, pp. 830–842.

Fulkerson, B., Vedaldi, A., and Soatto, S. (2008). Localizing objects with smart dictionaries, in *Proceedings 10th European Conference on Computer Vision, ECCV 2008*, pp. 179–192.

Funes Mora, K. A. and Odobez, J. (2012). Gaze estimation from multimodal kinect data, in *IEEE Computer Society Conference on Computer Vision and Pattern Recognition Workshops (CVPRW), 2012* (IEEE), pp. 25–30.

Funes Mora, K. A. and Odobez, J.-M. (2013). Person independent 3d gaze estimation from remote rgb-d cameras, in *International Conference on Image Processing, EPFL-CONF-192423* (IEEE).

Furukawa, Y. and Ponce, J. (2009). Accurate, dense, and robust multi-view stereopsis, *PAMI 2009*.

Gachery, S. and Magnenat-Thalmann, N. (2001). Designing mpeg-4 facial animation tables for web applications, MIRALab, University of Geneva.

Griffin, G., Holub, A., and Perona, P. (2007). Caltech-256 object category dataset, Tech. Rep. 7694, California Institute of Technology.

Gross, R., Matthews, I., Cohn, J., Kanade, T., and Baker, S. (2010). Multi-PIE, *Image and Vision Computing* **28**, 5, pp. 807–813.

Guestrin, E. D. and Eizenman, E. (2006). General theory of remote gaze estimation using the pupil center and corneal reflections, *IEEE Transactions on Biomedical Engineering* **53**, 6, pp. 1124–1133.

Hansen, D. W. and Ji, Q. (2010). In the eye of the beholder: A survey of models for eyes and gaze, *IEEE Transactions on Pattern Analysis and Machine Intelligence* **32**, 3, pp. 478–500.

Hartley, R. and Zisserman, A. (2003). *Multiple View Geometry in Computer Vision*, 2nd edn. (Cambridge University Press, New York, NY, USA).

Hofer, G. (2004). *Emotional speech synthesis*, Master's thesis, University of Edinburgh.

Hong, P., Wen, Z., and Huang, T. S. (2001). IFACE: A 3d synthetic talkingn face, *International Journal of Image and Graphics* **1**, 1, pp. 19–26.

Hong, P., Wen, Z., and Huang, T. S. (2002). Real-time speech-driven face animation with expressions using neural networks, *IEEE Transactions on Neural Networks* **13**, 4, pp. 916–927.

Hu, Y., Jiang, D., Yan, S., and Zhang, H. (2004a). Automatic 3d reconstruction for face recognition, *FGR2004*.

Hu, Y., Jiang, D., Yan, S., Zhang, L., and Zhang, H. (2004b). Automatic 3d reconstruction for face recognition, in *International Conference on Automatic Face and Gesture Recognition* (*FGR2004*).

Hu, Y., Zeng, Z., Yin, L., Wei, X., Tu, J., and Huang, T. S. (2008a). A study of non-frontal-view facial expressions recognition, in *International Conference on Pattern Recognition*.

Hu, Y., Zeng, Z., Yin, L., Wei, X., Zhou, X., and Huang, T. S. (2008b). Multi-view facial expression recognition, in *2008: 8th IEEE International Conference on Automatic Face and Gesture Recognition, FG 2008*.

Hu, Y., Zhang, Z., Xu, X., Fu, Y., and Huang, T. (2007). Building large scale 3d face database for face analysis, *MCAM2007*.

Huang, T. S., Hasegawa-Johnson, M. A., Chu, S. M., Zeng, Z., and Tang, H. (2009). Sensitive talking heads [applications corner], *IEEE Signal Processing Magazine* **26**, 4, pp. 67–72.

Iida, A. (2002). *Corpus-based speech synthesis with emotion*, Ph.D. thesis, University of Keio, Japan.

Jiang, D., Gao, W., and Wang, Z. L. Z. (2002). Animating arbitrary topology 3d facial model using the mpeg-4 facedeftables, in *In Proceedings of IEEE International Conference on Multi-modal Interface*, pp. 517–522.

Jiang, D., Hu, Y., and Yan, S. (2005). Efficient 3D reconstruction for face recognition, *Journal of Pattern Recognition* **38**, pp. 787–798, Special Issue on Image Understandings for Digital Photographs (PR2005).

Just, M. and Carpenter, P. (1976). Eye fixations and cognitive processes, *Cognitive Psychology* **8**, 4, pp. 441–480.

Khorrami, P., Le, V., Hart, J. C., and Huang, T. S. (2014). A system for monitoring the engagement of remote online students using eye gaze estimation, in *2014 IEEE International Conference on Multimedia and Expo Workshops (ICMEW)* (IEEE).

Kim, E. H., Hyun, K. H., Kim, S. H., and Kwak, Y. K. (2009). Improved emotion recognition with a novel speaker-independent feature, *IEEE/ASME Transactions on Mechatronics* **14**, 3, pp. 317–325.

Kshirsagar, S., Molet, T., and Magnenat-Thalmann, N. (2001). Principal components of expressive speech animation, in *Proceedings of International Conference on Computer Graphics*, pp. 38–44.

Langton, S., Honeyman, H., and Tessler, E. (2004). The influence of head contour and nose angle on the perception of eye-gaze direction, *Attention, Perception, & Psychophysics* **66**, 5, pp. 752–771.

Lazebnik, S. and Raginsky, M. (2009). Supervised learning of quantizer codebooks by information loss minimization, *IEEE Transactions on Pattern Analysis and Machine Intelligence* **31**, 7, pp. 1294–1309.

Lazebnik, S., Schmid, C., and Ponce, J. (2006). Beyond bags of features: Spatial pyramid matching for recognizing natural scene categories, in *Proceedings of the IEEE Computer Society Conference on Computer Vision and Pattern Recognition*, Vol. 2, pp. 2169–2178.

Le, V., Brandt, J., Lin, Z., Bourdev, L. D., and Huang, T. S. (2012). Interactive facial feature localization, in *ECCV* (3), pp. 679–692.

Le, V., Hu, Y., and Huang, T. (2009). A quantitative evaluation for 3d face reconstruction algs, *ICASSP2009*.

Levine, M. D. and Yu, Y. C. (2009). State-of-the-art of 3d facial reconstruction methods for face recognition based on a single 2D training image per person, *Pattern Recognition Letters* **30**, 10, pp. 908–913.

Lewis, J. P. and Pighin, F. (2006). Retargeting: algorithms for performance-driven animation, in *ACM SIGGRAPH 2006 Courses, SIGGRAPH'06* (ACM, New York, NY, USA).

Lian, X. C., Li, Z., Lu, B. L., and Zhang, L. (2010). Max-margin dictionary learning for multiclass image categorization, in *Proceedings 11th European Conference on Computer Vision — ECCV 2010*, Vol. 4, pp. 157–170.

Littlewort, G., Whitehill, J., Wu, T., Fasel, I., Frank, M., Movellan, J., and Bartlett, M. (2011). The computer expression recognition toolbox (cert), in *2011 IEEE International Conference on Automatic Face and Gesture Recognition and Workshops, FG 2011*, pp. 298–305.

Liu, C., Yuen, J., and Torralba, A. (2011). Sift flow: Dense correspondence across scenes and its applications, *IEEE Transactions on Pattern Analysis and Machine Intelligence* **33**, 5, pp. 978–994.

Lu, F., Sugano, Y., Okabe, T., and Sato, Y. (2011). Inferring human gaze from appearance via adaptive linear regression, in *IEEE International Conference on Computer Vision (ICCV)*, pp. 153–160.

Lucas, B. D. *et al.* (1981). An iterative image registration technique with an application to stereo vision, in *Proceedings of the 7th International Joint Conference on Artificial Intelligence.*

Lucey, S., Ashraf, A. B., and Cohen, J. F. (2007). Investigating spontaneous facial action recognition through AAM representations of the face, in K. Delac and M. Grgic (eds.), *Face Recognition* (I-Tech Education and Publishing), pp. 275–286.

Mairal, J., Bach, F., Ponce, J., Sapiro, G., and Zisserman, A. (2008). Discriminative learned dictionaries for local image analysis, in *26th IEEE Conference on Computer Vision and Pattern Recognition, CVPR.*

Mairal, J., Bach, F., Ponce, J., Sapiro, G., and Zisserman, A. (2009). Supervised dictionary learning, in *Proceedings of the 2008 Conference on Advances in Neural Information Processing Systems 21*, pp. 1033–1040.

Martins, F., de Oliveira, A. F., Dahmer, A., and Barreto, L. (2012). MonSys-Monitoring System for Students and Tutors of Postgraduate Courses of UNASUS/UFMA in Distance mode using Moodle.

Mazza, R. and Dimitrova, V. (2007). Coursevis: A graphical student monitoring tool for supporting instructors in web-based distance courses, *International Journal of Human–Computer Studies* **65**, 2, pp. 125–139.

McLaughlin, T., Cutler, L., and Coleman, D. (2011). Character rigging, deformations, and simulations in film and game production, in *ACM SIGGRAPH 2011 Courses, SIGGRAPH'11* (ACM, New York, NY, USA), pp. 5:1–5:18.

McMurrough, C. D., Metsis, V., Rich, J., and Makedon, F. (2012). An eye tracking dataset for point of gaze detection, in *Proceedings of the Symposium on Eye Tracking Research and Applications, ETRA'12* (ACM), pp. 305–308.

Merchant, J., Morrissette, R., and Porterfield, J. L. (1974). Remote measurement of eye direction allowing subject motion over one cubic foot of space, *IEEE Transactions on Biomedical Engineering* **4**, pp. 309–317.

Meyer, G. and Do, M. (2013). Real-time 3d face modeling with a commodity depth camera, in *2013 IEEE International Conference on Multimedia and Expo Workshops* (*ICMEW*), pp. 1–4, doi:10.1109/ICMEW.2013.6618317.

Mitchell, S. C., Bosch, J. G., Lelieveldt, B. P. F., van der Geest, R. J., Reiber, J. H. C., and Sonka, M. (2002). 3-D active appearance models: segmentation of cardiac mr and ultrasound images, *IEEE Transactions on Medical Imaging* **21**, 9, pp. 1167–1178.

Montero, J. M., Gutiérrez-Arriola, J., Colás, J., Macías-Guarasa, J., Enríquez, E., and Pardo, J. M. (1999). Development of an emotional speech synthesiser in Spanish, *Proceedings of Eurospeech'99.*

Moore, S. and Bowden, R. (2009). The effects of pose on facial expression recognition, in *British Machine Vision Conference.*

Moore, S. and Bowden, R. (2011). Local binary patterns for multi-view facial expression recognition, *Computer Vision and Image Understanding* **115**, 4, pp. 541–558.

Morimoto, C. H., Koons, D., Amir, A., and Flickner, M. (2000). Pupil detection and tracking using multiple light sources, *Image and Vision Computing* **18**, 4, pp. 331–335.

Murray, I. R. (1989). *Simulating emotion in synthetic speech*, Ph.D. thesis, University of Dundee, UK.

Nagesh, P. and Li, B. (2009). A compressive sensing approach for expression-invariant face recognition, in *IEEE Conference on Computer Vision and Pattern Recognition, 2009. CVPR 2009* (IEEE), pp. 1518–1525.

Netop (2013). Netop —- vision classroom management, http://www.netop.com/classroom-management-software/products/netop-vision.htm.

Nguyen, P., Fleureau, J., Chamaret, C., and Guillotel, P. (2013). Calibration-free gaze tracking using particle filter, in *IEEE International Conference on Multimedia and Expo (ICME)*, pp. 1–6, doi:10.1109/ICME.2013.6607532.

Ohno, T., Mukawa, N., and Yoshikawa, A. (2002). Freegaze: a gaze tracking system for everyday gaze interaction, in *Proceedings of the 2002 Symposium on Eye Tracking Research & Applications* (ACM), pp. 125–132.

Ostermann, J. (2002). *Face Animation in MPEG-4* (Wiley-Blackwell), pp. 17–56.

Pandzic, I. and Forchheimer, R. (eds.) (2002). *MPEG-4 Facial Animation* (Wiley, UK).

Pantic, M. and Bartlett, M. S. (2007). Machine analysis of facial expressions, in K. Delac and M. Grgic (eds.), *Face Recognition* (I-Tech Education and Publishing), pp. 377–416.

Park, U. and Jain, A. (2006). International workshop on video processing for security, in *Third Canadian Conference on Computer and Robot Vision (CRV'06)*, pp. 41–48.

Parke, F. I. (1972). Computer generated animation of faces, in *Proceedings of ACM National Conferences*, pp. 451–457.

Perronnin, F. (2008). Universal and adapted vocabularies for generic visual categorization, *IEEE Transactions on Pattern Analysis and Machine Intelligence* **30**, 7, pp. 1243–1256.

Phillips, P., Grother, P., Micheals, R., Blackburn, D., Tabassi, E., and Bone, M. (2003). Face recognition vendor test 2002, in *IEEE International Workshop on Analysis and Modeling of Faces and Gestures, 2003. AMFG 2003*, doi: 10.1109/AMFG.2003.1240822.

Pighin, F. and Lewis, J. P. (2006). Facial motion retargeting, in *ACM SIGGRAPH 2006 Courses, SIGGRAPH'06* (ACM, New York, NY, USA).

Pitrelli, J. F., Bakis, R., Eide, E. M., Fernandez, R., Hamza, W., and Picheny, M. A. (2006). The ibm expressive text-to-speech synthesis system for American english, *IEEE Transactions on Audio, Speech and Language Processing* **14**, 4, pp. 1099–1108.

Rara, H., Elhabian, S., Starr, T., and Farag, A. (2008). A statistical model combining shape and spherical harmonics for face reconstruction and recognition, in *Biomedical Engineering Conference, 2008. CIBEC 2008.* Cairo International, pp. 1–4, doi:10.1109/CIBEC.2008.4786037.

Romdhani, S., Blanz, V., and Vetter, T. (2002). Face identification by fitting a 3d morphable model using linear shape and texture error functions, in *European Conference on Computer Vision*, pp. 3–19.

Romdhani, S. and Vetter, T. (2003). Efficient, robust and accurate fitting of a 3d morphable model, in *Ninth IEEE International Conference on Computer Vision, 2003*, pp. 59–66 vol.1, doi:10.1109/ICCV.2003.1238314.

Rose, S. A., Djukic, A., Jankowski, J. J., Feldman, J. F., Fishman, I., and Valicenti-Mcdermott, M. (2013). Rett syndrome: an eye-tracking study of attention and recognition memory, *Developmental Medicine & Child Neurology* **55**, 4, pp. 364–371.

Rosten, E. and Drummond, T. (2005). Fusing points and lines for high performance tracking, in *Tenth IEEE International Conference on Computer Vision, 2005. ICCV 2005*, Vol. 2 (IEEE), pp. 1508–1515.

Rudovic, O., Patras, I., and Pantic, M. (2010a). Coupled gaussian process regression for pose-invariant facial expression recognition, in *Proceedings 11th European Conference on Computer Vision — ECCV 2010*, Vol. 2, pp. 350–363.

Rudovic, O., Patras, I., and Pantic, M. (2010b). Regression-based multi-view facial expression recognition, in *Proceedings of International Conference on Pattern Recognition*, pp. 4121–4124.

Sarris, N., Grammalidis, N., and Strintzis, M. (Oct. 2002). FAP extraction using three-dimensional motion estimation, *IEEE Transactions on Circuits and Systems for Video Technology* **12**, 10, pp. 865–876.

Schröder, M. (2004). *Speech and emotion research: an overview of research frameworks and a dimensional approach to emotional speech synthesis*, Ph.D thesis.

Schröder, M. and Grice, M. (2003). Expressing vocal effort in concatenative synthesis, in *Proceedings of the 15th International Conference on Phonetic*, pp. 2589–2592.

Shi, J. and Tomasi, C. (1994). Good features to track, in *1994 IEEE Conference on Computer Vision and Pattern Recognition (CVPR'94)*, pp. 593–600.

Shih, S.-W., Wu, Y.-T., and Liu, J. (2000). A calibration-free gaze tracking technique, in *Proceedings of 15th International Conference on Pattern Recognition, 2000*, Vol. 4 (IEEE), pp. 201–204.

Shotton, J., Johnson, M., and Cipolla, R. (2008). Semantic texton forests for image categorization and segmentation, in *26th IEEE Conference on Computer Vision and Pattern Recognition, CVPR*.

Smith, B., Yin, Q., Feiner, S., and Nayar, S. (2013). Gaze locking: passive eye contact detection for human–object interaction, in *ACM Symposium on User Interface Software and Technology (UIST)*, pp. 271–280.

Stockman, G. and Shapiro, L. (2001). *Computer Vision*, 1st edn. (Prentice-Hall PTR, Upper Saddle River, NJ, USA).

Stoneware (2011). Stoneware classroom management software, `http://www.stone-ware.com/lanschool/monitor`.

Sync, S. (2011). Smart sync classroom management software, `http://smarttech.com/Solutions/Education+Solutions/Products+for+education/Software/SMART+Sync`.

Taheri, S., Sankaranarayanan, A. C., and Chellappa, R. (2013). Joint albedo estimation and pose tracking from video, *IEEE Transactions on Pattern Analysis and Machine Intelligence* **35**, 7, pp. 1674–1689.

Tan, K.-H., Kriegman, D., and Ahuja, N. (2002). Appearance-based eye gaze estimation, in *Proceedings of Sixth IEEE Workshop on Applications of Computer Vision, 2002. (WACV 2002)* (IEEE), pp. 191–195.

Tang, H., Fu, Y., Tu, J., Hasegawa-Johnson, M., and Huang, T. S. (2008a). Humanoid audio-visual avatar with emotive text-to-speech synthesis, *IEEE Transactions on Multimedia* **10**, 6, pp. 969–981.

Tang, H., Fu, Y., Tu, J., Huang, T. S., and Hasegawa-Johnson, M. (2008b). Eava: A 3d emotive audio-visual avatar, in *2008 IEEE Workshop on Applications of Computer Vision (WACV'08)*.

Tang, H., Hasegawa-Johnson, M., and Huang, T. (2010). Non-frontal view facial expression recognition based on ergodic hidden Markov model supervectors, in *2010 IEEE International Conference on Multimedia and Expo, ICME 2010*, pp. 1202–1207.

Tang, H., Hu, Y., Fu, Y., Hasegawa-Johnson, M., and Huang, T. S. (2008c). Real-time conversion from a single 2D face image to a 3D text-driven emotive audio-visual avatar, in *2008 IEEE International Conference on Multimedia and Expo* (IEEE), pp. 1205–1208.

Tang, H. and Huang, T. (Oct. 2008). Mpeg4 performance-driven avatar via robust facial motion tracking, in *15th IEEE International Conference on Image Processing, 2008. ICIP 2008*, pp. 249–252.

Tang, H. and Huang, T. S. (2008a). 3D facial expression recognition based on automatically selected features, in *2008 IEEE Computer Society Conference on Computer Vision and Pattern Recognition Workshops, CVPR Workshops*.

Tang, H. and Huang, T. S. (2008b). 3D facial expression recognition based on properties of line segments connecting facial feature points, in *2008: 8th IEEE International Conference on Automatic Face and Gesture Recognition, FG 2008*.

Tang, H., Zhou, X., Odisio, M., Hasegawa-Johnson, M., and Huang, T. S. (2008d). Two-stage prosody prediction for emotional text-to-speech synthesis. in *Interspeech*, pp. 2138–2141.

Tao, H. and Huang, T. S. (1999). Explanation-based facial motion tracking using a piecewise Bézier volume deformation model, in *CVPR*, pp. 1611–1617.

Tariq, U. (2013). *Image-based facial expression recognition*, Ph.D. thesis, University of Illinois at Urbana-Champaign.

Tariq, U. and Huang, T. S. (2012). Features and fusion for expression recognition - a comparative analysis, in *IEEE Computer Society Conference on Computer Vision and Pattern Recognition Workshops*, pp. 146–152.

Tariq, U., Lin, K.-H., Li, Z., Zhou, X., Wang, Z., Le, V., Huang, T. S., Lv, X., and Han, T. X. (2012a). Recognizing emotions from an ensemble of features, *IEEE Transactions on Systems, Man, and Cybernetics, Part B: Cybernetics* **42**, 4, pp. 1017–1026.

Tariq, U., Yang, J., and Huang, T. (2012b). Multi-view facial expression recognition analysis with generic sparse coding feature, in *Proceedings of Workshops and Demonstrations on Computer Vision — ECCV 2012*, Vol. III (Berlin, Germany), pp. 578–88.

Tariq, U., Yang, J., and Huang, T. (2013). Maximum margin gmm learning for facial expression recognition, in *FGR 2013: (to appear in) Proceedings of the 10th International Conference on Automatic Face and Gesture Recognition.*

Tariq, U., Yang, J., and Huang, T. S. (2014). Supervised super-vector encoding for facial expression recognition, *Pattern Recognition Letters* **46**, pp. 89–95.

Tian, Y., Kanade, T., and Conn, J. F. (2001). Recognizing action units for facial expression analysis, *IEEE Transactions on Pattern Analysis and Machine Intelligence* **23**, 2, pp. 97–115.

Tomasi, C. and Kanade, T. (1992). Shape and motion from image streams under orthography: a factorization method, *International Journal of Computer Vision* **9**.

Tu, J., Tao, H., and Huang, T. (2007). Face as mouse through visual face tracking, *Computer Vision and Image Understanding* **108**, 12, pp. 35–40, Special Issue on Vision for Human–Computer Interaction.

Tu, J., Wen, Z., Tao, H., and Huang, T. (2003). Coding face at very low bit rate via visual face tracking, in *Proceedings of Picture Coding Symposium* (Citeseer), pp. 301–304.

Turk, M. and Pentland, A. (1991). Eigenfaces for recognition, *Journal of Cognitive Neuroscience* **3**, 1, pp. 71–86.

Underwood, G., Chapman, P., Brocklehurst, N., Underwood, J., and Crundall, D. (2003). Visual attention while driving: sequences of eye fixations made by experienced and novice drivers, *Ergonomics* **46**, 6, pp. 629–646.

Valenti, R., Sebe, N., and Gevers, T. (2012). Combining head pose and eye location information for gaze estimation, *IEEE Transactions on Image Processing* **21**, 2, pp. 802–815.

Valstar, M., Pantic, M., and Patras, I. (2004). Motion history for facial action detection in video, in *IEEE International Conference on Systems, Man and Cybernetics*, Vol. 1, pp. 635–640.

Valstar, M. F., Gunes, H., and Pantic, M. (2007). How to distinguish posed from spontaneous smiles using geometric features, in *Proceedings of the 9th International Conference on Multimodal Interfaces, ICMI'07*, pp. 38–45.

Wang, J., Yin, L., Wei, X., and Sun, Y. (2006). 3D facial expression recognition based on primitive surface feature distribution, in *2006 IEEE Computer Society Conference on Computer Vision and Pattern Recognition*, Vol. 2 (IEEE), pp. 1399–1406.

Weidenbacher, U., Layher, G., Strauss, P.-M., and Neumann, H. (2007). A comprehensive head pose and gaze database, in *3rd IET International Conference on Intelligent Environments, 2007. IE 07*, pp. 455–458.

Weise, T., Bouaziz, S., Li, H., and Pauly, M. (2011). Realtime performance-based facial animation, *ACM Transactions on Graphics (Proceedings SIGGRAPH 2011)*.

Wen, Z. and Huang, T. S. (2004). *3D Face Processing: Modeling, Analysis and Synthesis*, 1st edn. (Springer).

White, K. P., Hutchinson, T. E., and Carley, J. M. (1993). Spatially dynamic calibration of an eye-tracking system, *IEEE Transactions on Systems, Man and Cybernetics* **23**, 4, pp. 1162–1168.

Winn, J., Criminisi, A., and Minka, T. (2005). Object categorization by learned universal visual dictionary, in *Proceedings of the IEEE International Conference on Computer Vision*, Vol. II, pp. 1800–1807.

Wollaston, W. H. (1824). On the apparent direction of eyes in a portrait, *Philosophical Transactions of the Royal Society of London*, pp. 247–256.

Yang, J., Yu, K., and Huang, T. (2010). Supervised translation-invariant sparse coding, in *Proceedings of the IEEE Computer Society Conference on Computer Vision and Pattern Recognition*, pp. 3517–3524.

Yang, S. and Bhanu, B. (2011). Facial expression recognition using emotion avatar image, in *2011 IEEE International Conference on Automatic Face and Gesture Recognition and Workshops, FG 2011*, pp. 866–871.

Yin, L., Chen, X., Sun, Y., Worm, T., and Reale, M. (2008). A high-resolution 3d dynamic facial expression database, in *FG'08: 8th IEEE International Conference on Automatic Face Gesture Recognition, 2008*. pp. 1–6, doi: 10.1109/AFGR.2008.4813324.

Yin, L., Wei, X., Sun, Y., Wang, J., and Rosato, M. J. (2006). A 3d facial expression database for facial behavior research, in *FGR 2006: Proceedings of the 7th International Conference on Automatic Face and Gesture Recognition*, pp. 211–216.

Zeng, Z., Pantic, M., Roisman, G. I., and Huang, T. S. (2009). A survey of affect recognition methods: Audio, visual, and spontaneous expressions, *IEEE Transactions on Pattern Analysis and Machine Intelligence* **31**, 1, pp. 39–58.

Zhang, R., Tsai, P.-S., Cryer, J., and Shah, M. (1999). Shape-from-shading: a survey, *IEEE Transactions on Pattern Analysis and Machine Intelligence* **21**, 8, pp. 690–706, doi:10.1109/34.784284.

Zhang, W., Surve, A., Fern, X., and Dietterich, T. (2009). Learning non-redundant codebooks for classifying complex objects, in *Proceedings of the 26th International Conference on Machine Learning, ICML 2009*, pp. 1241–1248.

Zhang, Z., Hu, Y., Yu, T., and Huang, T. S. (2006). Minimum variance estimation of 3d face shape from multi-view, in *FGR 2006*.

Zheng, W., Tang, H., and Huang, T. S. (2012). Emotion recognition from non-frontal facial images, in A. Konar and A. Chakraborty (eds.), *Advances in Emotion Recognition* (Wiley).

Zheng, W., Tang, H., Lin, Z., and Huang, T. (2010). Emotion recognition from arbitrary view facial images, in *Proceedings 11th European Conference on Computer Vision ECCV 2010*, Vol. 6, pp. 490–503.

Zheng, W., Tang, H., Lin, Z., and Huang, T. S. (2009). A novel approach to expression recognition from non-frontal face images, in *Proceedings of the IEEE International Conference on Computer Vision*, pp. 1901–1908.

Zhou, X., Cui, N., Li, Z., Liang, F., and Huang, T. S. (2009). Hierarchical Gaussianization for image classification, in *Proceedings of the IEEE International Conference on Computer Vision*, pp. 1971–1977.

Zhou, X., Zhuang, X., Yan, S., Chang, S., Hasegawa-Johnson, M., and Huang, T. S. (2008). Sift-bag kernel for video event analysis, in *MM'08 — Proceedings of the 2008 ACM International Conference on Multimedia, with Co-located Symposium and Workshops*, pp. 229–238.

Zhu, Z. and Ji, Q. (2004). Eye and gaze tracking for interactive graphic display, *Machine Vision and Applications* **15**, 3, pp. 139–148.

Zhu, Z. and Ji, Q. (2007). Novel eye gaze tracking techniques under natural head movement, *IEEE Transactions on Biomedical Engineering* **54**, 12, pp. 2246–2260.

Zhu, Z., Ji, Q., and Bennett, K. P. (2006). Nonlinear eye gaze mapping function estimation via support vector regression, in *18th International Conference on Pattern Recognition, 2006. ICPR 2006*, Vol. 1 (IEEE), pp. 1132–1135.

Zorrilla, M. E. and Álvarez, E. (2008). Matep: Monitoring and analysis tool for e-learning platforms, in *Eighth IEEE International Conference on Advanced Learning Technologies, 2008. ICALT'08* (IEEE), pp. 611–613.

Index

Q

R

S